ASIA IN THE TWENTY-FIRST CENTURY

ECONOMIC,
SOCIO-POLITICAL,
DIPLOMATIC ISSUES

ECONOMIC IDEAS LEADING TO THE 21ST CENTURY

edited by Lawrence Klein *(University of Pennsylvania)* and
Vincent Su *(Baruch College, CUNY)*

Vol. 1: The Japanese Economy
Mitsuo Saito

Vol. 2: Asia in the Twenty-First Century:
Economic, Socio-Political and Diplomatic Issues
edited by Paula Chow and Gregory Chow

Vol. 3: Who Shall Live? Health, Economics, and Social Choice (2nd edition)
Victor R. Fuchs

Vol. 4: India's Economic Prospects: A Macroeconomic and Econometric Analysis
Thampy Mammen

Economic Ideas Leading to the 21st Century — Vol. 2

ASIA IN THE TWENTY-FIRST CENTURY

ECONOMIC, SOCIO-POLITICAL, DIPLOMATIC ISSUES

Editors

Paula K. Chow
International Center, Princeton University

Gregory C. Chow
Department of Economics, Princeton University

World Scientific
Singapore • New Jersey • London • Hong Kong

Published by

World Scientific Publishing Co. Pte. Ltd.

P O Box 128, Farrer Road, Singapore 912805

USA office: Suite 1B, 1060 Main Street, River Edge, NJ 07661

UK office: 57 Shelton Street, Covent Garden, London WC2H 9HE

British Library Cataloguing-in-Publication Data
A catalogue record for this book is available from the British Library.

First published 1997
Reprinted 1999

ASIA IN THE TWENTY-FIRST CENTURY:
Economic, Socio-Political and Diplomatic Issues

ISBN 981-02-3034-6

Printed in Singapore by Uto-Print

Foreword

This series is intended to appeal to both the general reader and the professional economist. The selected titles will be quantitative, for the most part, and based on broadly accepted economic doctrine. No particular "school of thought" will be emphasized, but existing economic policies, histories, and analytic methods will be presented. In general, the subjects dealt with will be quantitative and applicable to the world around us.

Modern institutions and methods of reasoning will be emphasized. A number of books dealing with the awakening and expansion of notable economies of Asia will be prominent, but quite different types of books will also appear in the series. The new information sources and techniques that are being developed in these waning days of the twentieth century will be used by several authors in the series. Our aim will be to encourage people to use and understand the methods involved. That is the main sense in which this series will be intended to take economists into the 21st century.

It is evident that books about specific economies will be featured in this series — Japan, the Republic of Korea, China, and India will be examined with a firm eye by economists. These cases stand as attractive beacons for other aspiring writers about specific economies. It is to be hoped, and it is intended, however, that a significant series can be generated in this way, to show how much has been accomplished in East Asia during the closing two decades of the 20th century.

Paula and Gregory Chow have put together a timely volume that fits very well with this series. They have assembled the deep thinking of Princetonians to elucidate economic issues of China. This is one of the focal subjects for the whole series, and they have been extremely perceptive in seeking some of the best ideas on the subject.

May 1997 Lawrence R. Klein

Preface

The idea of a conference on Asia in the twenty-first century to celebrate Princeton University's 250th anniversary was conceived by Paula Chow and Bob McCartney on the bus ride to the Peking Airport at the end of an Alumni College on the Chinese Economy on July 22, 1993. After observing the dynamic economic development during a three-week trip to China beginning with Hong Kong, participants were excited about the events in Asia and agreed that such a conference would be of general interest. After discussion with colleagues in Princeton, several options were open concerning the format of the Conference. One was to open the Conference to a wider audience in Hong Kong. The option finally chosen was to limit the participation to Princeton alumni and friends. The event was jointly sponsored by the International Center and the Alumni Council of Princeton University. Douglas Blair of the Alumni Council and Paula Chow of the International Center cooperated in the planning and running of the Conference. They received significant ideas and generous support from Ivy Wu, Michael Morgan, Doria Lee and Robert Glicksman in Hong Kong and Knut Hammerskjold of International Alumni of Princeton.

The Conference took place at the Marriot Hotel in Hong Kong on Friday and Saturday, April 19 and 20, 1996. Two half-day sessions on Friday covered economic and social-political issues respectively, while the session on Saturday dealt with U.S.–Asia relations. Because of the broad scope of the subject only East and South-east Asia were represented, and regrettably, even some important countries in the region were not sufficiently covered. The speakers were mainly Princeton alumni who are active players in and near the area. One notable exception is Dr. Xie Xide, former President of Fudan University who visited Princeton in the early 1980's to establish relations between Fudan and Princeton and has since visited Princeton several times. We could not have asked a better person to present the issues from China's perspective. The moderators for the three sessions were respectively Gregory Chow of the Economics Department, Gil Rozman of the Sociology Department and William Atwell, an alumnus on the faculty of Ohio State University. Luther Munford, Chairman of the Alumni Council, opened the Conference. Gordon Wu, President of the Princeton Club of Hong Kong and honorary chairman of the Conference, made several speeches to welcome the participants and introduce some speakers. Harold Shapiro, President of Princeton University, also gave several speeches, including one on the relevance of the American development experience to the development of technology in Asia. We were fortunate to have Luther Munford who served as Master of Ceremonies present a bird's eye view of the Conference from Princeton's perspective. The Conference is considered an activity of the Alumni Council.

Over two hundred and fifty alumni and friends from seventeen countries with classes spanning a 66-year period attended the Conference. The presentations were of high quality, as the reader can judge by reading the chapters included in this volume. The participants were able to share the knowledge and experience of a group of distinguished alumni who are active players in Asia affairs. There was plenty of time for questions and comments from the floor, making the Conference an interactive experience. The speakers and other participants have different national and cultural backgrounds and represent different points of view. For example, in discussing U.S.–Asia relations James Baker represented an American viewpoint whereas in the same session Yoshio Hatano represented a Japanese point of view, as did Toyoo Gyohten in a different session on economic issues. Yet all speakers shared a Princeton experience and spoke as members of the Princeton family. They spoke openly and had a great deal of respect for one another's viewpoints. It was truly an exciting and educational experience for all concerned. We therefore decided to edit a volume of these papers so that others, within and outside the Princeton community, can share this experience as well.

We would like to thank Professor Lawrence Klein for including this book as a volume in the series he is editing, Anne Dropick and Jesse Traub for editing the manuscript, and David Marshall and Amanda Terry for providing a tape reading of the speeches, including the one by Stapleton Roy on which Chapter 14 was based. In the preparation of the manuscript, Cynthia Cohen has provided excellent assistance for which we would like to express our many thanks.

Paula K. Chow
Gregory C. Chow

Contents

The Contributors

L. Desaix Anderson, Jr.
Charge d'Affaires, Embassy of the USA
Hanoi, Vietnam

James A. Baker, III
Former US Secretary of State;
Trustee, Princeton University;
Senior Partner, Baker and Botts L.L.P.
Texas, USA

Nelson An-Ping Chang
President, Chia Hsin Cement;
President, Princeton Club of Taiwan
Taipei, Taiwan

Gregory C. Chow
Class of 1913 Professor of Political Economy
Princeton University
New Jersey, USA

Paula K. Chow
Director, International Center
Princeton University
New Jersey, USA

Richard K. Eu
Chairman, Singapore Institute of
Management Advisory Council;
Chairman, LC Developments
Singapore, Republic of Singapore

Toyoo Gyohten
Senior Advisor, The Bank of Tokyo-Mitsubishi, Ltd;
President, Institute for International Monetary Affairs;
President, Princeton Club of Japan
Tokyo, Japan

Bae Ho Hahn
President, The Sejong Institute
Seoul, Korea

Yoshio Hatano
Former Ambassador to the UN
Tokyo, Japan

John T. Kamm
Principal, Kamm and Associates
California, USA

Tsu-Koon Koh
Chief Minister of Penang
Penang, Malaysia

Gill-Chin Lim
Professor, Michigan State University
Michigan, USA

Berry Metzger
General Counsel, Asian Development Bank
Manila, Philippines

Luther T. Munford
Chair, Princeton University Alumni Council;
Partner, Phelps, Dunbard L.L.P.
Mississippi, USA

J. Stapleton Roy
US Ambassador to Indonesia;
Former US Ambassador to China
Jakarta, Indonesia

Harold T. Shapiro
President, Princeton University
New Jersey, USA

Xie Xide
President Emeritus, Fudan University
Shanghai, People's Republic of China

PART I

ECONOMIC ISSUES

Chapter 1

Introduction

Gregory C. Chow and *Paula K. Chow*

This volume consists of papers presented before the Conference on Asia in the 21st Century which took place in Hong Kong on April 19 and 20, 1996 to celebrate Princeton University's 250th Anniversary. The papers were presented by Princeton alumni, with the exception of Chapter 9. The subject matter is of general interest as Asia, together with North America and Europe, is assuming a leadership role in world affairs. Any internationally-minded person can benefit from reading this book. The coverage is by no means complete. Yet the excitement of the conference and the expertise of the authors that are revealed in the papers will compensate for the lack of complete coverage. The reader will obtain accounts of important facts as well as a balanced perspective in understanding events that are taking place in East Asia.

The book is organized in four parts, the first three reflect the content of the conference which deals with economic and socio-political issues and U.S.–Asia relations; and the fourth part deals with Princeton's perspectives on the Conference. Gregory Chow, moderator of the first session, provided the following opening remarks:

"We Princetonians are proud to celebrate the 250th Anniversary of our University. World history is defined in terms of only several thousand years and Princeton has lived through a quarter of a thousand years. We are proud of our heritage, but we look forward to the future, as we get together to discuss the 21st Century. We recognize the important role Asia will play in the next century and have selected Asia in the 21st Century as the topic of our conference. We meet here in Hong Kong, an economic center of Asia to discuss this topic in three respects. First economic, second, social-political and third, relations between the U.S. and Asia. This morning our panelists will look at the economic changes in Asia from several different perspectives. We are fortunate to have had the paper by Toyoo Gyohten to give an excellent introduction. First, Eugene Wong, Vice-President of the Hong Kong University of Science and Technology in charge of Research and Development, will discuss technology in economic development. Second, Nelson Chang, President of Chia-Hsin Cement in Taiwan, provides a viewpoint as a successful entrepreneur. Third, Tsu-Koon Koh, Chief Minister of Penang, Malaysia, will speak on the economy of Penang. Fourth, Barry Metzger, General Counsel of the Asia Development Bank will address the issues of poverty in Asia's economic development. Finally, Nick Hope, Director of the China and Mongolia Division of the World Bank, will serve as moderator for the discussion led by Mr. Koh and Mr. Metzger and give his perspective as an administrator of the World Bank. We are very fortunate to have the expertise and experiences of these distinguished Alumni."

Chapter 2, drawn from a keynote speech by Toyoo Gyohten, deals with Japan's growing partnership role in Asia. It provides an interesting and important perspective from a Japanese, and to some extent, an Asian point of view. The presentation led the moderator of the first session to remark, after hearing the speech, that this speech alone was worth a four-day round-trip from Princeton to Hong Kong to attend the Conference, as he could use it for his Monday lecture at Princeton.

Nelson Chang, a leading entrepreneur of international businesses with a home in Taiwan, discussed the changing tides in global economic development as recorded in Chapter 3. From this informative and well-organized chapter, the reader can obtain a bird's eye view on the growing importance of Asia in the world's economy, in comparison with Europe, the United States and other developing countries. Nelson writes with the confidence and excitement of a successful Asian entrepreneur.

To balance the positive and optimistic view about Asia's development, the reader can benefit from reading about the poverty issues in developing countries as presented in Chapter 4 by Barry Metzger, legal adviser in the Asia Development Bank. A discussion of the problems associated with poverty and suggestions for possible solution were presented.

Tsu-Koon Koh, Minister of Penang, Malaysia, records for us in Chapter 5 the successful experience of the economic development of the city which he administers. He has been responsible for many of the successful economic policies discussed. Nicholas Hope, head of the China and Mongolian Division of the World Bank in Washington, D.C., presented some remarks on China's economic development. Since his remarks on China's development are too brief for a chapter, we fill the gap by including in Chapter 6 a paper by Gregory Chow on China's economic development and its challenges to Europe, originally presented at Forum Engelberg held in Engelberg, Switzerland, on Europe-Asia economic and technological cooperation. This is the only article included which was not presented at the Conference. The editors felt there was not sufficient material on China.

The session on socio-political issues was moderated by Gil Rozman. Its first paper, recorded in Chapter 7, deals with human rights issues in China. Its author, John Kamm, has done more than any other American in helping political prisoners in China to obtain their human rights; and has been responsible for persuading the Chinese authorities to release a number of well-known political prisoners. His chapter is informal in style, giving the reader a taste of the atmosphere in which he spoke, but commands the attention of the audience and reader.

Richard Eu, a leader of the business community in Singapore, is well qualified to discuss its economic and social development in Chapter 8. Americans are often critical of Singapore for its very strict rules on economic, political and social behaviors of its citizens. Many of its citizens prefer such a system to one with more freedom and more crime. Such preference is shared by many Asians. Richard's account provides us with useful information to assess the economic and social development of his country.

The Conference participants and the readers are fortunate to have the contribution by Xie Xide on social and economic reform in Shanghai in Chapter 9. This chapter deals with four important aspects of economic reform: privatization of residential housing, unemployment problems of migrant workers, social insurance and uneven rates of growth in coastal and interior provinces of China. It also discusses political reforms briefly. Like other important players in China's reform process, the author speaks from a pragmatic, problem-solving point of view. Understanding this viewpoint is important for understanding the recent developments in China.

Chapter 10 by Bae Ho Hahn, President of the Sejong Institute, is concerned with political and social change in Korea. As Korea is perhaps even less understood than Japan and China among many of the readers the chapter is a useful contribution to this volume. In it the reader will learn how significant political leaders ruled Korea and how social changes were made. This chapter ends Part II of the volume.

Part III on U.S.–Asia relations begins in Chapter 11 with a major speech by former Secretary of State, James Baker, on U.S. policy toward Asia. It deals with U.S. policies toward Russia, Japan and China. It is a statesman-like address, stimulating to the audience. Gill-chin Lim, a University Professor at Michigan State University, provides an interesting and insightful discussion of values in U.S.–Asian relations in Chapter 12. It gives a very different perspective from the political discourse of the previous chapter.

Our current ambassadorial representative to Vietnam, Desaix Anderson, and our former ambassador to China and current ambassador to Indonesia, Stapleton Roy, are most qualified to address U.S. relations in these respective countries. Chapter 13 on Vietnam not only deals with U.S. policy toward that country but provides an informative and concise account of its economic development. From that account, one can draw many parallels between China's reform process (see Chapter 6) and Vietnam's. One gets a sense that Vietnam is in the process of succeeding in its reform and development, as China has succeeded. The statements on U.S. policy are authoritative. Chapter 14 summarizes the valuable experience of a seasoned diplomat who has been stationed in China and Indonesia. It tells us not only about U.S. relations but also the political, economic, and cultural background of these countries under which our policy operates. The author's remarks about China and Indonesia are penetrating, and will greatly enhance our understanding of the social, economic and political reality of these countries, their economic successes, and the problems they face. On the basis of a deeper understanding, our ambassador suggests that we can formulate a more realistic and less idealistic foreign policy towards these and other Asian countries.

Chapter 15, the last chapter of Part III is authored by Yoshio Hatano on Japan's foreign policy. Like Chapter 11 on America's Asian policy by Baker, Hatano's chapter is an address by a former policy maker as the author served as the Japanese ambassador to the United Nations. It represents a Japanese viewpoint in as much as Chapter 11 represents an American viewpoint. The free expressions and exchanges by active participants and best-informed observers are what made the Conference in Hong Kong an exciting experience. It is hoped that readers of this volume can share this exciting experience as well.

In Part IV, which is concerned with Princeton University's perspective of the Conference, we are fortunate to have President Shapiro contribute chapter 16 entitled "Princeton and Asia in the Twenty-first Century" and Luther Munford, Chairman of the Alumni Council, contribute the next chapter entitled "Alumni Gather in Hong Kong to Discuss Asia's Future". These two chapters are different in nature from the rest of the book in that they do not deal with the issues in Asia per se, but add clarity to the readers' understanding on the importance of the Conference from the point of view of Princeton University.

Chapter 2

Japan's Growing Partnership Role in Asia

Toyoo Gyohten

The end of the Cold War has brought about major political and economic changes of global scale. Under the Cold War regime the confrontation was between democracy and market economy on one side and socialism and centrally-planned economy on the other. West and East, under the leadership of the U.S. and the Soviet Union respectively, created a status of confrontation and antagonism between them. However, it was true that a certain degree of order and stability was maintained within each camp. The end of the Cold War marked the end of confrontation and antagonism but it also implied an end of order and stability.

At the end of World War II in 1945 the world political and economic order was faced with a historic challenge. Fortunately, the world did succeed in establishing, almost immediately, a new global order called Bretton Woods regime. Under the regime the world economy could launch a process of development with guiding principles such as expansion of free trade, stability of international monetary system, and assistance to the developing world. Multilateral institutions including IMF, World Bank and GATT played a leading role.

Unfortunately, at the end of the Cold War today we see no hope that we will have a new global order comparable with Bretton Woods. I can cite several causes of our inability. The most important one is the fact that we now do not have the U.S. of 1945. In 1945 the U.S. was the dominant economic, political, military, and cultural power willing and capable of assuming the global leadership role. The rest of the world was more or less prepared to accept the U.S. initiative. Although the U.S. today is still the most powerful country in the world, particularly after the disintegration of the Soviet Union, her hegemonic clout is no longer comparable to what she had in 1945. Another important cause was the change of national policy-priority. As the result of the end of the Cold War the ideological confrontation between East and West disappeared and the nightmare of World War III disappeared. Yet the extinction of the ideological conflict between nations triggered the renewed recognition of the importance of economic competition. Governments and peoples are obliged to pay greater attention to their own economic competitiveness and welfare. It was this shift in the national policy priority which prompted many countries in the world to seek certain regional alliances among those with common economic interest in order to strengthen their bargaining power. In hindsight, the acceleration of the European integration and the creation of NAFTA in the late 80's were episodes which reflected the new global trend in the post-Cold War period.

Against the backdrop as such, it has become a popular argument that the twenty-first century will be the century of Asia. Indeed, the U.S. has lost her overwhelming economic and political dominance. Europe is undergoing arduous political and economic adjustment in the aftermath of the collapse of the Soviet Union and the unification of two Germanys; and is still unable to replay the historic role of the Great Europe. However, the recent eminence of Asia was created not only by the relative decline of the traditional great powers; but also by the remarkable economic development during the last 20 years or so, covering Japan, Asian NIEs, ASEAN and China.

The development of East Asia was certainly not accomplished overnight. In the 1960's Japan became a focus of global attention as an emerging economic power catching up with the U.S. and Europe. It was soon followed by Asian NIEs, i.e. Korea, Taiwan, Singapore and Hong Kong. Following them, ASEAN countries came to realize their vast potential for dynamic progress. Then, China started a giant stride. In other words, in East Asia, one country after another has played the role of a forerunner, pulling the rapid economic growth of the entire region. They look like a group of youthful and virile runners dashing up a hill. The world was struck with awe and amazement. This is the single most important factor behind the rapid ascendance of Asia on the global scene.

There are four major elements which contributed to the phenomenal economic development of East Asia:

1. In most countries of East Asia there is a strong national aspiration toward development which is shared not only by the government but also by the vast majority of the people.
2. In the process of realization of the national aspiration, public sector and the private business sector successfully maintained an efficient cooperative division of labor and established an export-oriented industrial structure. With few exceptions, East Asian governments demonstrated enlightened leadership with a right set of policy objectives. At the same time, there was a market-oriented private sector dynamism with abundant innovative entrepreneurship. Two sectors did not confront each other, rather they supported each other.
3. Most East Asian countries enjoyed a high savings ratio, which enabled vigorous accumulation of domestic capital. Also, in general, labor ethics were sound, which generated high labor productivity.
4. East Asia could enjoy favorable external support. In the first place the U.S. provided a vast open market for the East Asian exports. It was also the U.S. which guaranteed the security of the region. Since the 1980's Japan stimulated East Asian economic development by supplying capital, technology and managerial know-how.

The phenomenal development of East Asia attracted attention from outside the region. It was inevitable that the attention included a certain sense of alarm. Also it was natural that East Asia, although hesitantly, grew self-assertive recognizing the greater role it was playing in the global economy.

The most important factor which heightened the outside world's interest in East Asia was the desire to participate in the fast growing East Asian market. The U.S. was the first country to realize the importance of East Asia. While the relation between the U.S. and East Asia has a long history there was not a period like the one of the last 10 years or so when East Asia became such an important trading partner. The year 1983 was a historic one for the U.S. and East Asia. It was the year when U.S. exports to East Asia exceeded its exports to Latin America. In the same year the trans-Pacific trade of the U.S. surpassed its trans-Atlantic trade. Today the trans-Pacific trade is 50 percent larger than the trans-Atlantic trade. In 1980 the share of exports to EU in total U.S. exports was 24 percent. Ten years later in 1990 it remained almost unchanged at 25 percent. On the other hand, the share of East Asia in total U.S. exports was 20 percent in 1980 but it grew to 27 percent in 1990, exceeding EU. Similar development took place for imports. The share of EU in total U.S. imports was 15 percent in 1980 and increased slightly to 18 percent in 1990. The share of East Asia in the total U.S. imports exploded from 25 percent in 1980 to 37 percent in 1990. These figures eloquently demonstrate how important East Asia is for the U.S. today.

East Asia's importance for EU has also increased. In spite of the strong historical tie across the Atlantic, EU's exports to East Asia exceeded exports to the U.S. for the first time in 1992.

The growing trade relationship with East Asia was clearly a crucial backdrop of the greatly enhanced interest in East Asia on the part of non-regional developed countries. In particular, the concept of Asia-Pacific was assiduously promoted by the U.S., Australia, and Canada. Their enthusiasm was instrumental in the creation of APEC.

APEC is indeed a quite significant regional arrangement. With its current membership APEC represents 38.4 percent of the world population, 53 percent of the world GNP and 41.3 percent of the world trade. Intra-regional economic flows in APEC are also quite impressive. The share of intra-regional exports in APEC's total is 66.0 percent and that of imports is 67.2 percent. These ratios are higher than the comparable ratios for EU, i.e. 61.3 percent and 59.3 percent respectively.

As to the capital flow in the region, most of the foreign capital inflow into East Asian countries in older days was from the U.S. and Europe. Later, Japanese investment became important. A significant change took place during the last 10 years in this respect as well. Intra-regional investment among East Asian countries increased prominently. The greatest contributor to the enhanced intraregional capital flow was from Chinese investors who live outside mainland China. Today overseas Chinese capital from Hong Kong, Taiwan, Singapore, Malaysia, etc. is pouring into Mainland China and other East Asian countries. In 1994, of the total direct investment made in East Asian countries, about two-third's, $50 billion, came from the region.

Such descriptions may sound almost euphoric about the future development of the Asian economy. However, I have to caution that there are still many risks in store for the future of Asia.

1. The phenomenal development of the Asian economy so far has been very much dependent upon the inflow of foreign capital, technology, and management which were successfully combined with the abundant supply of inexpensive labor in the host countries. As long as the supply of these resources are available, the Asian economy will continue to grow at a reasonably high rate. However, it is quite likely that sooner or later the supply will taper off. Then in order to continue growth on a more self-sustained basis, it will be critically important for the region to develop indigenous technology with which to produce competitive goods and services to capture the global market. It is indeed a big challenge for the region.
2. As is well known, direct investment has been by far the most important form of foreign capital inflow into Asia. During the period 1990-1994 the share of direct investment was 45 percent of the total capital inflow to Asia while the comparable number

for Latin America was 30 percent, and for all developing countries 37 percent. Indeed, direct investment is a favorable type of capital inflow because it is a kind of non-debt capital flow, and also it is accompanied by technological transfer in most cases. When it is export-oriented investment, it contributes to the strengthening of the host country's foreign currency earning capacity in a relatively short span of time.

However, the strength of direct investment has its own risk. It cannot be denied because of the ample supply of direct investment, the development of the domestic market for long-term capital has lagged. This was the case, in particular, for the primary market for bonds and stocks. It should also be noted that, in many countries in the region, local private banks are not functioning effectively in mobilizing and channeling stable long-term capital in the domestic market.

3. Well-established social infrastructures, particularly in such areas as legal system, tax codes, labor practice etc. are indispensable for balanced and sustainable economic development. It cannot be denied that some countries in the region still have a long way to go in this respect.
4. Political and social stability are crucial conditions for successful economic development. At the same time, one can argue that it is not too difficult to maintain political and social stability when the living standard of the society is rising rapidly. When the speed of economic growth inevitably slows down, it will become important for the society to have had matured enough so that it can be open to the outside and can accept internal diversity.
5. Environmental deterioration is a great risk for Asia. If the dynamism of Asian economic growth is concentrated on quantitative physical development then the outcome can be irrecoverable destruction of the environment. This is the last thing that Asia should ignore. Also, equally important issues will include effective control of the population and good management of the consumption of food and energy.

6. We should not forget that Asia is the largest importer of arms. Every effort is needed to improve the security of the environment so that the pressure of defense expenditure does not weaken fiscal balance and distort resource allocation.
7. The key word for Asia is diversity. It is quite different from the homogeneity of the EU and the unipolarity of NAFTA. That is, Asia has to live with the inherent instability in its balance of power structure. It is impossible for a single organization. either ASEAN or APEC, to deal with all the problems in the region. Therefore it is more than natural to see several countries in the region that have issues of common interest creating a forum to discuss those issues among themselves. I would argue that it could be even desirable and necessary to have a set of multilayered and overlapping fora as such within the region as long as they are non-discriminatory. Such structure will contribute to the stability and flexibility of the framework of APEC. It goes without saying that a matter of fundamental importance for the stability of the region is the maintenance of a cooperative and nonconfrontational triangular relationship between the U.S., China and Japan. Any crack in the triangle will immediately generate serious uncertainty, not only for the security of the region but also for the sustained economic development of the entire region.

So far I have discussed risks and challenges for Asia. There is no question that in the area of the economy, politics and security Asia will be playing a leading role for the world in the twenty-first century. In addition, however, I would strongly hope that Asia would provide for us a unique opportunity to create a new set of values for the world. After the end of the Cold War everyone proclaimed support for democracy and market economy. At the same time, however, we came to recognize that there are different kinds of democracy and market economy. Market economy is made up of a variety of factors, and the question is which factor should be considered most important. The pursuit of efficiency through free competition is certainly one important factor. As we see in the U.S., the society which relentlessly pursues efficiency and free competition tends to become a society where every deal must be sealed in a written contract and every dispute must be settled through lawyers. On the other hand, there are market economies where people emphasize more the value of equality and compromise. For them the best way to gain efficiency is to avoid waste as the result of excessive competition. The reason why we often hear a comparative analysis of the American model, Continental European model, Asian model, Japanese model, etc. is that people are seriously seeking the best model to fit their conditions and are exploring the best standard of value upon which economic management should be based in order to achieve the highest welfare for the greatest numbers of the society.

Asia can provide the best forum for this exercise because it is a region of diversity. In the framework of APEC we can exchange views on different standards of value and can learn that there will never be only a single value standard which is right. Through this process we may be able to establish our value standard which is best for the society and which at the same time shares international compatibility.

Now, what is the role which Japan can and should play in Asia? Historically, Japan's involvement in Asia has undergone changes over time. Until the early decades of the 20th century, Japan played a representative role of reviving Asia, particularly in the face of expanding Western imperialism. The rapid emergence of Japan as a modern industrialized state attracted global attention to Asia. However, since the 1930's, under growing dominance of militaristic chauvinism in the nation, Japan turned itself into a late-coming imperialist. It launched aggression in other parts of Asia and eventually trapped itself in a suicidal war against the Allied powers. During 15 years, until the defeat in 1945, the criminal acts committed by Japan in some Asian countries left a lasting scar on Japan's relations with Asia. Japan will have to carry the burden of atonement for years to come.

Since 1945 Japan's involvement with Asia marked a new era. It has been the history of a rapidly growing economic tie based on amicable political relations and steady exchange of people and culture. By the 1960's Japan more or less completed its economic recovery from the wartime destruction and the establishment of a democratic political and social system. The strong national aspiration toward development, the effective combination of government leadership and private entrepreneurship, rapid internalization of imported technology, and the development of indigenous technology and managerial skill, and above all, hardworking and thrifty people were main factors which enabled the Japanese success. There is no question that many Asian countries recognized that at least some of these factors were usefully incorporated in their own development strategy.

In the early stage, the trade structure between Japan and Asia was vertical: namely, Japan imported raw materials and exported manufactured goods. Japan's investment in Asia was mainly for the purpose of extracting raw materials. However, as an increasing number of labor-intensive industries in Japan became less competitive as the result of rising wages and an appreciating yen, the Japanese manufacturing industry began to transfer production to other Asian countries. Also, Asian manufactured products with competitive prices and quality penetrated the Japanese market. In other words, trade became more horizontal. In response to the rising level of the technological skill of many Asian countries and their desire to have high-tech industries, Japanese direct investments in Asia shifted more to those of technology-intensive type. The horizontal division of labor in Asia will expand. It is true that trade between Japan and the rest of Asia is still marked by a large surplus on the Japanese side. In my view, it was made inevitable, to a considerable extent, by the fact that many of the joint ventures set up by Japanese and local business still require imports of capital goods from Japan. However, I am sure the situation will improve as the ability of the local industry improves.

On the financial side Japan remains in possession of the largest accumulation of investible financial resources. Japan has been running a current account surplus in excess of $100 billion per year for four consecutive years. It is Japan's important role to recycle financial resources to the rest of the world. Through a variety of forms including ODA, direct investment, portfolio investment, and bank loans, Japan has been actively playing a role. It is noteworthy that the share of Asia in capital markets has steadily increased during the last decade. Japan has been making efforts to render its financial market more accessible and make the yen a more usable international currency. All in all, the process of the integration of the Japanese economy with the rest of Asia is steadily proceeding.

I must not forget to mention that the economic integration must be accompanied by an active interchange of people and culture between countries. The process of mutual learning cannot be complete if it happens only in the economic arena.

As I repeatedly stressed the keyword for Asia is diversity. It will be a serious mistake if we try to summarize Asia as a single homogeneous group. Japan is clearly part of Asia, but it is different from others just as each Asian country is different from others. Therefore, it is wrong to try to describe the relation between Japan and Asia by simply juxtaposing Japan on one side and all the rest of Asia on the other. Japan's relation with Asia is multilateral. Asia consists of a network of mutual dependence and mutual benefit. However, one common ingredient which is shared by all Asians and which makes Asia different from other regions in the world is the aspiration toward development, the respect for hard work and the spirit of cooperation rather than confrontation. Japan is not able to be and does not want to become a hegemonic power in Asia. We know our own limitations. What Japan wants to do and believes it can do is to remain as a partner who stimulates and supports development and shares the benefit of common achievement.

Chapter 3

Changing Tides in Global Economic Development

Nelson An-ping Chang

Since the end of the Cold War following the seemingly overnight collapse of the Soviet Union, the world is undergoing changes of seismic magnitude. The Warsaw Pact has essentially disintegrated. At the same time, the influence of the United States on the western alliance has undoubtedly weakened. We are witnessing vast transfers of world power along with fundamental transformations of global political and economic systems. The world is moving from a bipolar conflict situation to a pluralistic, multipolar new world order/ disorder. People now demand more say on political, social and economic issues. On the positive side, democracy in one form or another has become a norm of social and political changes. Market economies have also noticeably been replacing centrally planned economies. Deregulation and privatization have become popular trends in most parts of the world. On the negative side, we are again seeing pre-World War I-style ethnic and regional rivalries and religious confrontations. The world has not yet reached a post Cold War strategic equilibrium. Worst of all, the world has little group consensus, along with an absence of effective world or regional leadership.

Under this uncertainty, the world is moving toward the escalation of inward-looking regionalism. Many countries are going regional in order to hedge their bets. UNESCAP estimates that there are at least several dozen such groupings now. The best-known groupings are the European Union (EU), the North American Free Trade Agreement (NAFTA) and the ASEAN Free Trade Area (AFTA). All of these are regional trading-blocs in nature. There are also other regional groupings, less of the trading-bloc type, such as the Asia-Pacific Economic Cooperation group (APEC), the Pacific Economic Cooperation Council (PECC) and the Pacific Basin Economic Council (PBEC). They have been formed to facilitate and to promote regional cooperation in trade and investment and for better utilization of resources. There are also political groupings such as the Council for Security Cooperation of Asia and the Pacific (CSCAP) and the ASEAN Regional Forum (ARF), etc. This intensification of regional, sub-regional and bilateral/ "regionalateral" preferential agreements has raised growing concerns about their compatibility with future global system such as GATT and the WTO. Each region has its own priorities.

Over the past few years, the 17 Asia-Pacific members of APEC have excluded Europe. In February 1996, the Asia-Europe Meeting (ASEM) met in Bangkok without the participation of the United States. Only the seven ASEAN countries, the PRC, Japan, South Korea and the EU's 15 countries are members. From this development, it is clear that the Asia-Pacific region is the focus of the world. Both the United States' and Europe's economic policies and political strategies are no longer Euro-focus and US-centric.

The center of gravity for the world economy has apparently shifted from Europe and North America to the Asia-Pacific region. However, the region has an enormous diversity of countries. Economic, cultural and political systems differ dramatically, not only from capitalism to socialism, but also including a wide variety of competing forms of capitalism. Within this region are the most intense trade conflicts. Luckily, Asia-Pacific nations' economic activities are quintessentially global rather than regional in scope and composition. Global economic engagement still remains the fundamental interest of every member of this region.

Since the mid-1980s, the Asia-Pacific region has benefited enormously from economic liberalization and deregulation. It has been experiencing continued high economic growth. The most recent estimate of 7.4 percent growth for 1996 again tops the world (Exhibit 1). Japan today already has a per capita income larger than that of the United States and Germany.* At the same time, the per-capita incomes of the ROC, Hong Kong and Singapore are larger than those of Spain, Portugal and Greece (Exhibits II, III, IV). The Asia-Pacific region already produces a third of world vehicle output, a third of world computer output, a quarter of world steel output and two-thirds of the world's consumer electronics products. In 1995, Taiwan was the third largest "information product" supplier in the world, behind only the United States and Japan. According to the OECD's estimate, by the year 2040 Asia's manufacturing output will account for 50 percent of total world output, as against only around 25 percent today. No wonder, according to the newest "World Competitiveness Report" prepared by the World Economic Forum and Swiss Management School IMA, most Asian countries rank higher than, or at least equal to, European or North American countries in competitiveness. On the consumption side, according to John Gray, the Chairman of Hong Kong Bank, Asia will have over one billion middle-class consumers by the year 2100. Most of these consumers will be easily reached across a few densely-populated Asian market centers (Exhibit V).

The three main driving forces behind Asia are prevalent education, a high-quality labor force and fast regional integration. At the same time almost all Asian countries emphasize macroeconomic stability. Their governments have exercised a fiscal discipline that sets an example for the private sector. Today's savings rates are approximately 50 percent higher than elsewhere (Exhibit Vl). A regional contagion effect is also taking place, from Japan to the newly-industrialized economies (NIEs), and from the NIEs to the rest of the Asian developing countries. Funds, technologies and ideas transfer actively within Asia.

* This calculation is based on current market exchange rates for converting income into a common currency unit for comparability among nations, but if purchasing-power-parity rates (PPP) are used, Japan's per capita income is not the largest.

Exhibit I

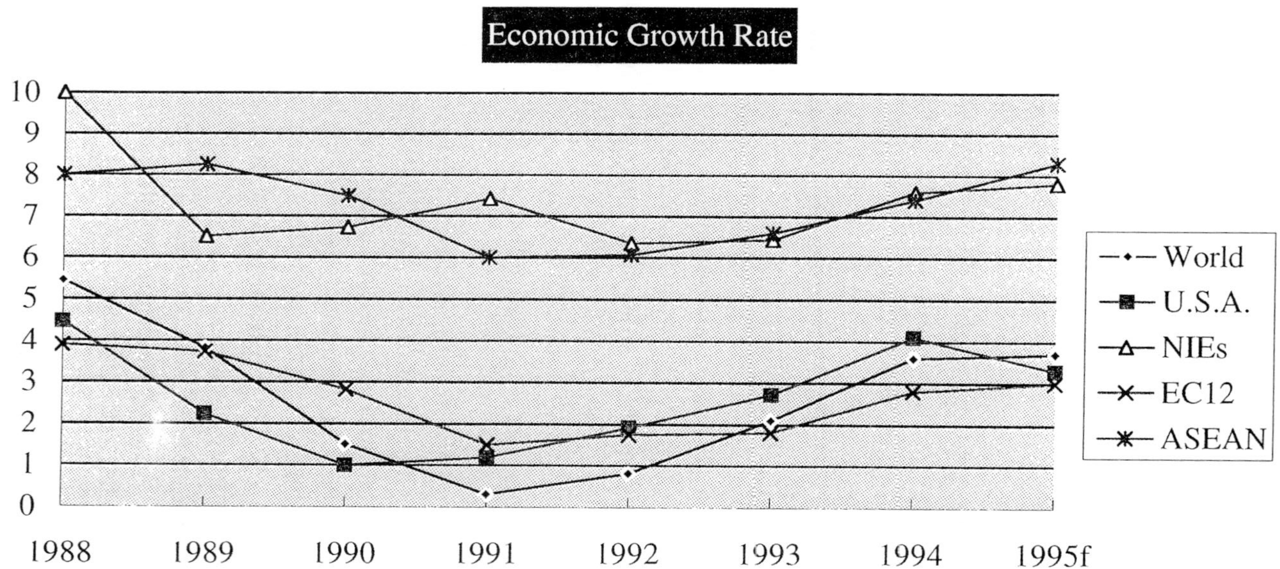

Source : International Financial Statistics (IMF)

Exhibit II

COMPARISON OF ECONOMIC STRENGTH (1994)

EC12 (Unit:US$ billion)

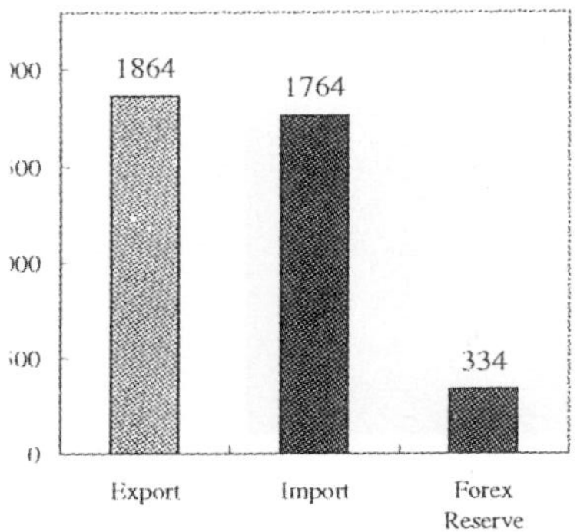

GNP=6,824

ASIA (Unit:US$ billion)

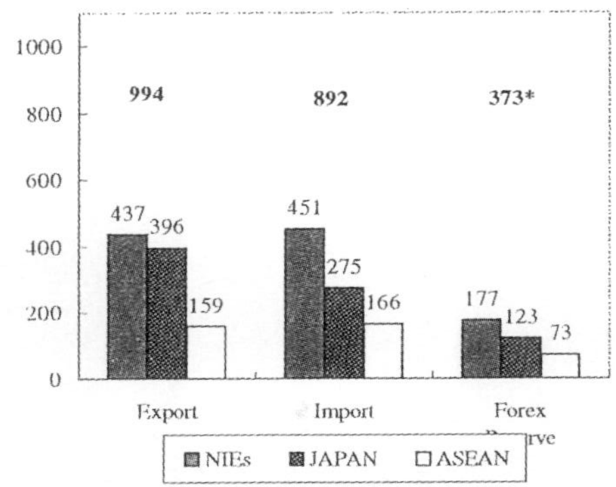

GNP=6,369

ASIA : Japan, South Korea, North Korea, Singapore, H.K., PRC, Indonesia, Malaysia, Philippines, and Thailand

*Forex Reserve of NIEs excludes H.K.

U.S. (Unit:US$ billion)

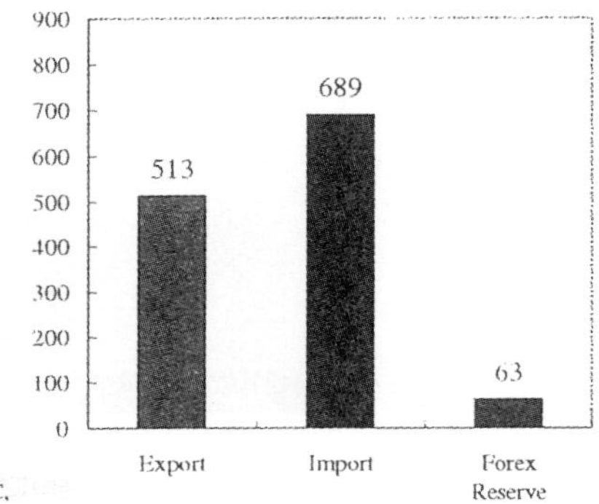

GNP=6,738

Source : (1) Main Economic Indicators, OECD, January 1996
(2) International Financial Statistics, January 1996

Exhibit III

Share of World Exports (%)

	1988	1991	1994	2000f
NIEs	8.40	8.80	10.06	15.61
ASEAN	2.60	2.80	3.62	5.56
PRC	1.60	1.80	2.79	4.89
JAPAN	9.40	9.13	9.14	9.47
U.S.A.	11.96	12.25	11.80	15.02
EU12	12.16	27.00	38.38	45.30
other countries	53.88	38.22	24.21	4.16

Source: International Financial Statistics, February 1996

Breakdown of World Exports, 1994

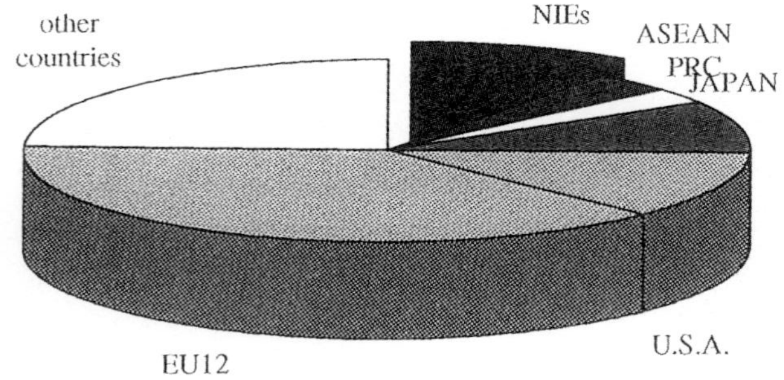

Breakdown of World Exports, 2000f

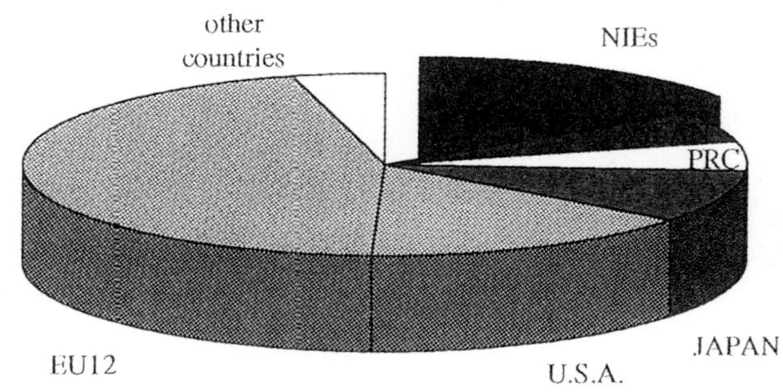

Exhibit IV

Share of World Imports (%)

	1988	1991	1994	2000f
NIEs	6.80	8.80	10.60	16.45
ASEAN	1.90	3.20	3.95	6.06
PRC	1.60	2.00	2.71	4.75
JAPAN	6.40	6.70	6.45	6.69
U.S.A.	16.56	14.23	16.16	20.57
EU12	27.30	28.00	31.60	37.29
other countries	39.44	37.07	28.53	8.19

Source: International Financial Statistics, February 1996

Breakdown of World Imports, 1994

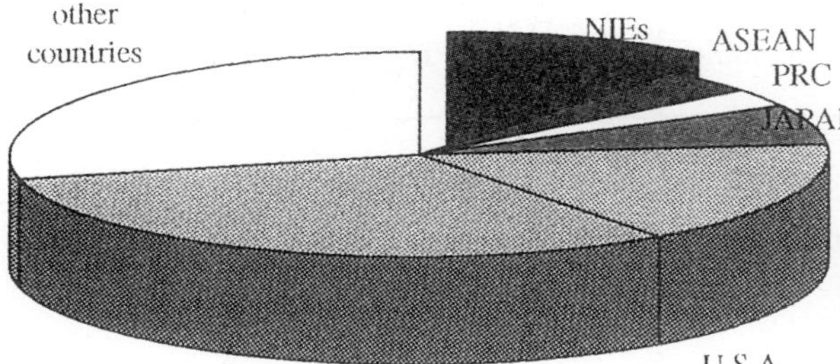

Breakdown of World Imports, 2000f

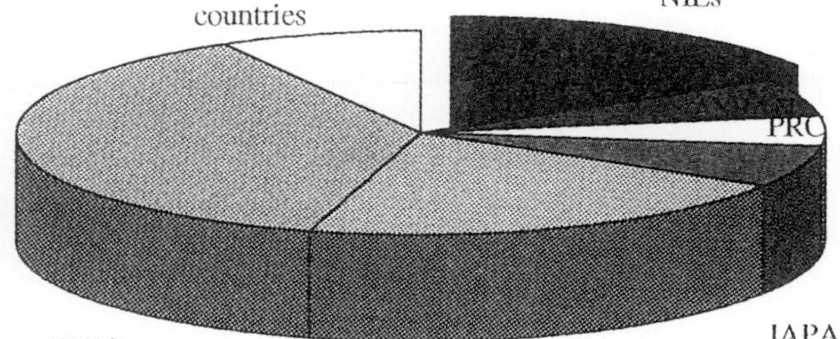

Exhibit V

Economic Size of Countries, 1994 & 2000(f)

Year	1994				2000f	
	GNP* (US$ bn)	Per Capita GNP* (US$)	Population (millions)	GNP Growth (%)	GNP** (US$ bn)	Per Capita GNP** (US$)
ROC	244	11,597	21.04	6.02	347	16,468
U.S.	6,738	25,816	260.65	4.10	8,046	30,826
EU12**	6,824	19,547	349.09	2.70	8,053	23,069
Japan	4,159	33,266	125.03	0.50	4,311	34,480
NIEs	823	9,663	74.57	7.60	1,277	14,996
ASEAN	408	1,332	337.71	7.40	626	2,044
PRC	508	424	1,203.00	11.80	891	743

Note: *: **Figures are at constant 1991 prices.**

: **Year 2000 figures are forecasted based on a constant annual compound GNP growth rates between 1994 and 2000. (U.S., Japan and PRC are based on a constant annual compound growth rates 3.0%, 0.6% and 9.8% respectively.)

Exhibit VI

East Asia savings are now impressive, allowing rapid economic growth
Gross Domestic Savings (% of GDP)

	Average 1971–80	1990	1994
NIEs:			
Hong Kong	27.50	33.30	31.10
South Korea	22.30	32.30	35.65
Singapore	30.00	42.40	44.70
ROC	32.20	30.00	27.30
NIEs average	28.00	34.50	31.30
ASEAN:			
Indonesia	22.60	35.70	38.70
Malaysia	30.40	31.40	33.00
Philippines	23.40	18.70	14.50
Thailand	21.50	28.20	35.00
ASEAN average	24.50	28.50	33.00
PRC	32.50	34.50	39.40
India	20.50	20.50	25.60
Japan	31.90	34.10	32.20#
U.S.	19.60	15.10	13.70
EU12	22.90	21.60*	22.40**

***data for 1989**
#data for 1993
****data for 1993, and not including U.K., Denmark, Luxembourg, Portugal**
Saving Rate = (National Income – Private consumption) / GDP; tax is included.
Source: (1) Asia Development Outlook 1994
(2) International Financial Statistics, January 1996

Exhibit VII

Intra-Regional Trade Trend, 1980, 1994, 2000f (Unit: US$ Billlion)

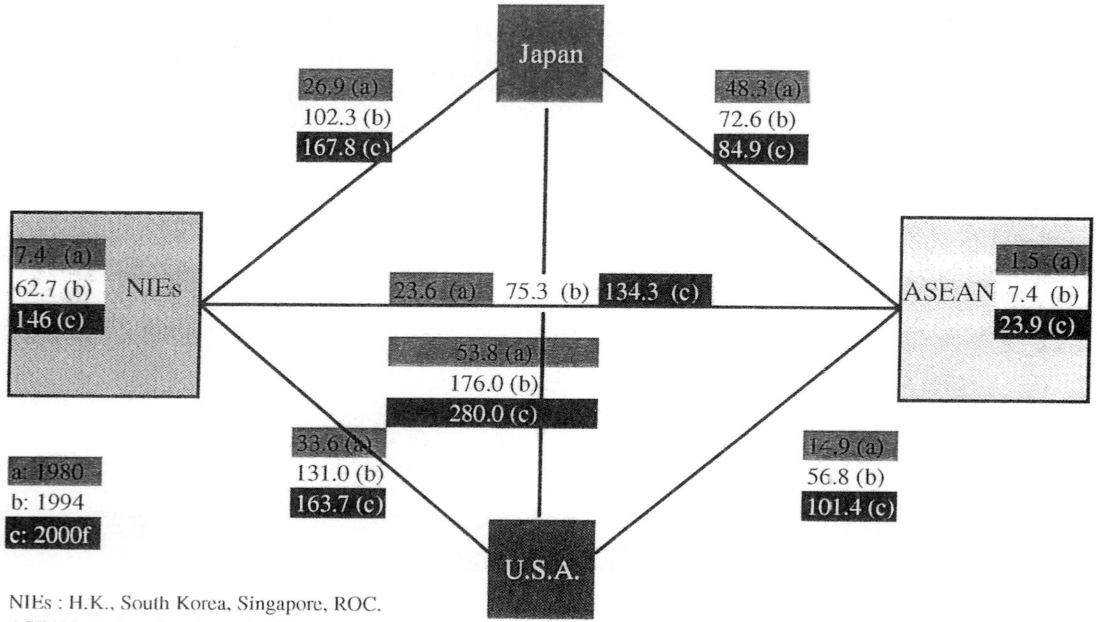

NIEs : H.K., South Korea, Singapore, ROC.
ASEAN : Indonesia, Malaysia, Philippines, Thailand.
Source : Direction of Trade Statistics, June 1995.

In the last few years, the Chinese Economic Area has also emerged as a new growth center for global trade and investment. In 1994, Taiwan saw an approximately 40 percent increase in exports to the PRC, and South Korea saw an approximately 150 percent increase in exports to the PRC. In fact, intra-Asia trade was growing at 30 percent per annum during the 1980s; during the first half of the 1990s, this growth figure increased over 40 percent. Intra-regional trade already well exceeded 40 percent of the total trade of these countries (Exhibit VII).

Economic and political changes in the Asian landscape are occurring at breathtaking speed. Challenges to the region's stability and prosperity are also enormous. Asian countries largely rely on exports for their economic growth. In the past 25 years, Japan has continued its economic strategy of effectively exporting unemployment, causing huge disequilibrium in international trade and capital flow. Now, the PRC's trade imbalance is second only to Japan's. In 1980 it was US$2 billion. By 1995 it grew to over US$30 billion. All Asian countries are following similar strategies, by encouraging exports. This inherently results in an intensification of trade conflicts and economic disputes in the region. These clashes reflect serious substantive problems. The volume of transactions is now so large that conflict over a small percentage can produce significant impacts. Trade conflicts can have similar or even more powerful "contagion effects". Trade conflicts can attain high political profiles which impede resolutions, adversely affect overall relations within the region, and cause repercussions on innocent bystanders. The warning lights are flashing.

We can no longer talk only about the relative performances of nations. The old national boundaries are becoming principally extraneous and dysfunctional for economic development. Current forces are so powerful that they are carving out new maps which supersede existing political or sovereign borders. However, there is a dangerous tendency to ignore multilateral mechanisms despite a growing pluralism of economic and political capabilities. Such a tendency runs counter directly to the economic and political realities of the world. The reality is that economic and political power is increasingly diffused across a growing number of economies. This diffusion along with growing interdependence requires new, collective and cooperative arrangements to manage international affairs, (i.e.) a multilateral form of decision-making and collective leadership.

Trade should not be a threat but a glue that strengthens international relationships. Intolerance and separatism will result in aggressive unilateralism and in attempts to manage trade which could undermine the global trading system.

On the economic side, despite continued conflicts, Asia will still be the center of attention of world trade and investment. However, on the political side, Asia is bursting with uncertainties. There are territorial disputes around Ryukyu Islands in the East China Sea, Spratly Islands in the South China Sea and Kuril Islands in the Sea of the Okhotsk, to name just a few. The main problem still remains between the PRC and Taiwan, a conflict which came to the center of world attention early this year. There is also no apparent solution between North and South Korea. After a brief contact in the early 1990s, tension seems to be mounting again in the Korean peninsula. In addition to local Asian problems, the United States would still like to assert its influence in Asia in order to maintain regional stability and economic opportunities. Maneuvers of U.S. aircraft carrier task forces in Asia during this year's Taiwan Straits tensions demonstrated that. Great Britain would also like to play an important role in Asia after the return of Hong Kong to the PRC in 1997. This is evidenced by joint military exercises between Great Britain and the Philippines. There are countless visible as well as invisible hands at play in the Asian political arena. The whole situation can be best described as strategic ambiguity.

In John Naisbitt's new book *Megatrends Asia,* he points out without reservation that Asia will be the principal driving force in world economic development in the twenty-first century. This presents both challenges and opportunities for Asian and non-Asian entrepreneurs. As reported in a recent issue of *Asian Business* (January 1996) David Li of the (Hong Kong) Bank of East Asia identified four key interdependent challenges to Asian entrepreneurs: (1) the generation gap between youth and experience; (2) cultural conflicts in companies expanding across cultures; (3) conflicts of values, (i.e.) traditional values vs. modern values; and (4) the arrival of the Information Age. The change in Asian enterprises is immense, from relatively simple domestic operations to multinational. For non-Asian companies, it is important to know that the growing interdependence in Asia has flowed largely from the activities of the private sector. It is essential for Western companies to tap into the Asian business network, especially the so-called Chinese network, with mutually beneficial Asian partners.

At the cusp of a new millennium, Asia's exceptional growth and economic dynamism offer unprecedented promises to the rest of the world. With economic issues at the top of the international agenda, we must aim for collective and cooperative responses to global problems. Multiregional cooperation and responsibility-sharing are the only ways to reach the final goal of a global village and prosperity for all mankind. Entrepreneurs must discard their notions from the previous centuries and adapt to this world flux. Asia now stands at a historical point which presents both opportunities and challenges. This colossal potential can be realized only by laying the foundation now.

Chapter 4

Economic Change in Asia

Barry Metzger

Many of us have been students of, and participants in, what is so often described as "the East Asia Miracle". When I first began working in Asia almost 30 years ago as a young American lawyer, the region (if it is ever possible to generalize about the "Asian region" as a whole) was the scene of military conflicts and civil instability, and poverty was pervasive. Informed analysts, looking at the region, were then concerned about the military scenarios, about the "domino effect" and about feeding Asia. The writing of Malthus, Sun Tze, Mao Tse-tung and General Giap were more on the minds of people than the writings of Adam Smith or other proponents of private enterprise and global trade.

In contrast, we now speak daily about the "East Asia Miracle", about developing countries with remarkably dynamic economies which, in some cases, have attained levels of per capita income that exceed those of major European nations which were once colonial masters. South Korea prepares for admission to the Organization for Economic Cooperation and Development (OECD), the "rich nations' club". Enterprises based in China have their shares traded on the New York Stock Exchange.

As a group, Asian developing economies have grown faster than those in other developing regions by a factor of at least *two.* In the eight-year period between 1987–1995, Asia experienced average GDP growth of 7.6 percent compared to a 2.3 percent average in Africa and a 2.5 percent average in Latin America and the Caribbean.

The contrast is even more pronounced when the growth of per capita income across developing regions is compared. Most other developing regions have experienced low or stagnant growth (and in the case of Africa, negative growth) in per capita income. In a notable exception to this trend, over the last two decades, per capita income in the Asian region has grown on the average by five percent per annum.

However, there are several problems with popular perceptions of the East Asia Miracle and in drawing inferences from the Asia-wide data which I have cited. First, both those popular perceptions and these figures mask the diversity in the performance of the various subregions and individual countries. Second, comparisons of average growth rates do not adequately capture the incidence of "absolute" or "relative" poverty across and within developing regions.

The Asian growth experience across subregions is *heterogeneous*. The aggregate growth rate of the region as a whole is pulled up by the exceptional growth performance of the new industrializing economies (NIEs) and the People's Republic of China (PRC). In the 1990's, South-east Asian economies have also succeeded in accelerating their growth rates, bringing them close to the region's average. While all NIEs have maintained high growth rates, some South-east Asian countries such as the Philippines and others have not done well. Performance of the South Asia subregion has also been consistently below average for the Asian region.

Per capita income of the South Asian economies have grown at a sluggish pace. Differences within the Asian region become even more apparent when levels of per capita income are examined. According to 1993 estimates, while the NIEs had per capita income of around $8,000 or more, the PRC, despite rapid growth of per capita income since the early 1980s, had a per capita income of about $500. Similarly, there is considerable diversity in per capita income among East Asian countries. In this subregion, four countries have meager per capita incomes: Cambodia, Lao People's Democratic

Republic (Lao PDR), Mongolia, and Vietnam. Low per capita incomes are also the norm in South Asia.

South Asian and the low-income East Asian countries are among the poorest in the world in terms of per capita income. Contrary to popular perception, if South Africa is excluded, the average per capita income of South Asia is no higher than that of sub-Saharan Africa,[1] and the average per capita income of poorer East Asian economies is considerably lower than that of sub-Sahara Africa.

Average per capita income in Latin America, the Middle East, and the European and Central Asian developing countries were two to three times greater than the average East Asian per capita income, and six to nine times more than that of South Asian.

If we take $1 per day as a poverty line at 1985-purchasing-power-parity exchange rates, then in 1990 (the last year for which such estimates are available), 59 percent of South Asia's population was below the poverty line. This is worse than East Asia (15 percent), Latin America (28 percent), the Middle East and North Africa (three percent), and even sub-Saharan Africa (53 percent). On this basis, South Asia has the highest global incidence of poverty. If the poverty line is increased to $2 per day at 1985-purchasing-power-parity exchange rates, approximately 90 percent of South Asia's population and 80 percent of sub-Saharan Africa's population live in poverty. It should be noted, however, that these estimates pertain to 1990, and, given the movement of per capita incomes in the two subregions over the last five years, the difference in the incidence of poverty in South Asia and sub-Saharan Africa has probably narrowed since then.

The total number of poor people in Asian countries is considerably higher than that of sub-Saharan Africa or, for that matter, any other developing region. According to rough estimates, South Asia alone has about 660 million people currently living in poverty, exceeding the total number of poor people in sub-Saharan Africa

[1] This is also reflected in the private per capita consumption level, which in 1993 was $320 in sub-Sahara Africa compared to $240 in South Asia.

and Latin America combined, which is estimated at about 350 million. Given the situation in such countries as Cambodia, PRC, Lao PDR, Mongolia, Myanmar and Vietnam, the total number of poor people in low-income Asia would be substantially higher than 660 million.

Asia is home to a majority of the world's poor and, in some parts of Asia, their situation is worse than that in the region commonly perceived as the poorest in the world — sub-Saharan Africa.

In recent years, there has been a sharp increase in net external resource flows into DMCs. In the four years prior to the recession in the industrial countries (1987–1990), long-term net inflows into the Asian region averaged $31 billion per annum. Since 1991, net inflows have averaged $75 billion per annum, peaking in 1994 at $109 billion and accounting for roughly half the net external resource inflows into the developing world. Private capital has dominated these inflows, accounting for 75 percent of the region's net external inflows during 1991–1994.

The bulk (or 82 percent) of the net resource inflows into the region in the 1990s went to a handful of countries — Indonesia, PRC, Korea, Malaysia, Philippines, and Thailand — mainly in the form of direct foreign investment and portfolio equity investment. In contrast, the poorer Asian economies have been dependent largely on official sources of finance. Among the poorer developing countries of Asia, only PRC, India and, to some extent, Pakistan were able to attract significant amounts of private capital. The PRC is the only low-income developing country within the region that has continued, so far, to attract private capital on a sustained basis.

The meager savings rates of the low-income developing countries in Asia constrain the investment that they can undertake from internally generated resources. With the limited availability of external resources (largely in the form of official finance), their rates of investment are also low, which in turn limits the rate of income growth. These economies are currently caught in a vicious trap of low and stagnant per capita incomes with a high incidence of poverty.

Development is about people: their education, their health and their wealth, and about their ability to realize their potential. Euphoria over the success of the Asian Tigers and the exhilarating pace of the commercial marketplace in Hong Kong, Singapore and other capitals should not obscure our vision of the broader realities within the region — the region which I have described as home to a majority of the world's poor. Much economic development within the region remains to be achieved, and there is much to be done.

Chapter 5

Economic Transformation of Penang, Malaysia

Tsu-Koon Koh

Historical Background

Penang's economic success today dates back two and a half decades ago when the State Government launched a bold plan to industrialize the State. The Penang economy at that time was based on entrepot trade and agriculture.

The industrialization program was initiated in the 1970s and intensified in the 1980s and the 1990s. Through pragmatism and dynamism, the government succeeded in stimulating growth and development of a totally new sector — the manufacturing sector — which remains the main engine of growth of the Penang economy. The manufacturing sector now accounts for 54 percent of the State's Gross Domestic Product (GDP) and employs over 49 percent of Penang's workforce.

Through the manufacturing sector, Penang has enjoyed sustainable, rapid and robust growth with annual growth rates averaging eight percent in the 1970s and 1980s and exceeding 12 percent in the 1990s. As growth gathered momentum in 1990–1995, Penang underwent an intensive and impressive process of industrial and technological transformation towards more technology–intensive, skill–intensive and capital–intensive production processes.

In the process, Penang has not only maintained its leadership position in the semiconductor electronics industry, but has moved into new areas, such as disk drives, computer parts and components, communication and consumer electronics of higher technological levels, precision metal parts, automated equipment and machinery.

Partners in Progress

In Penang, the government believes in working with the private sector and the people in its development programs, bringing to practice the call of "government of the people, for the people and by the people". The private sector on its part has risen to the occasion and provides valuable feedback to the government on its needs and expectations. Even at the policy formulating stage, the government consults with the private sector through industry and business groups. Implementation, therefore, becomes less problematic, in that almost everyone has ownership of the plans that are eventually drawn up and implemented.

The government plays the role of stimulating growth by providing incentives, infrastructure, regulations or deregulations, and a conducive environment for business to operate. It is perhaps this proactive and pro-business nature of the government that has contributed largely to the success story of Penang.

Reasons for Success

There are many factors that have contributed to Penang's success story in bringing about an industrial and economic transformation.

Electronics Boom

Penang's attempt at promoting investments in labor-intensive industries in the early 1970s to overcome its serious unemployment problem was well timed in that Penang caught the electronics boom of the West. It was also at that time that large American multinational corporations (MNCs) on the west coast of the U.S.A. were looking for offshore locations to locate their simpler and more labour intensive processes in order to be more cost effective.

Of the seven pioneer companies that started operations in Penang in 1972, all were involved in electronics. In fact, they were in the semiconductor industry, using relatively cheap but highly trainable labour.

Thus the electronics industry came to Malaysia through Penang, and today the country is one of the world's largest exporters of semiconductors and the third largest world producer, after the U.S.A. and Japan.

Incentives for Investments

The Malaysian government provides attractive tax incentive packages for projects to ensure that start-up and operating costs for the companies are competitive. Among the major incentives are:

* Pioneer Status
  A company granted Pioneer Status will enjoy partial exemption from the payment of income tax, for a period of up to five years. Only 30 percent of its statutory income is taxed. The government may consider granting a 100 percent exemption to strategic projects of national importance, which involve heavy capital investment, high technology which can generate extensive linkages.
* Investment Tax Allowance
  Companies may be granted an allowance of 60 percent of qualifed capital expenditure incurred within five years from the date of approval of the project. The allowance can be utilized to offset against 70 percent of statutory income in the year of assessment. Unutilized allowances can be carried forward to subsequent years, until the whole amount is used up. 30 percent of the statutory income will be taxed at the prevailing company tax rate.
* Reinvestment Allowance
  This is granted to companies which incur qualifying capital expenditure for the expansion of production capacity, modernisation and upgrading of production facilities and diversification into related products. The allowance is up to

60 percent of capital expenditure incurred by the companies, and can be used to offset 70 percent of the statutory income in the year of assessment.

There are also special incentives for:

Export credit refinancing
Industrial building allowance
Research and development
Training and teaching facilities
Operational headquarters

Infrastructure and Utilities

The industrialization program launched in the 1970s benefitted from the infrastructure already in place in Penang as a result of the State's former role as an entrepot port, serving to export the primary products produced by the various states of Malaysia and the surrounding hinterland, as well as to import manufactured goods and machinery for use by the country and the neighbouring areas. Seaport, airport, road and rail facilities were relatively well developed. Electricity, water and telecommunications were adequate. Services such as banking, insurance and freight forwarding were in place.

As a result of the successful industrialization program, the government has since upgraded the infrastructure facilities and the utilities to meet the discerning needs of industries.

* Port Facilities
  Penang port is strategically located at the entrance of the Straits of Malacca, a busy sea route linking the Indian Ocean to the Far East. As the second largest port in Malaysia, Penang offers modern facilities to international and coastal vessels, and is positioning itself as the premier port for the Indonesia-Malaysia-Thailand Growth Triangle (IMT GT) and the Bay of Bengal. Facilities in the port of Penang include a deep water wharf, a newly constructed container terminal and a bulk cargo terminal.

* Air Links
  Penang International Airport, the second largest in Malaysia, caters to the needs of wide-bodied jet liners and air cargo carriers. It has direct links with major cities in Asia. Its air cargo terminal serves several major carriers, such as Fed-Ex, Eva Air, China Airlines, Martinair, KLM, Lufthansa and Korean Airline. To allow for future growth a larger regional international airport is being planned.
* Highways and Railway
  Penang is situated at the crossroads of two major highways, the North-South Highway and the East-West Highway. The 13.5-km Penang Bridge, the longest in Asia, connects Penang Island to the Malaysian Peninsula. Construction of several additional major highways commenced in late 1996, while upgrading of the public transport and traffic systems is being planned to improve traffic flow and road transportation.

  Penang is connected by rail in the south to the capital city of Kuala Lumpur and Singapore and in the north to Bangkok.
* Electricity
  Adequate electric power is supplied by Tenaga Nasional Berhad (the national electric company) through the national grid system and the Prai and Glugor power stations in Penang, and is augmented by several independent power producers. The transmission and distribution systems are constantly being expanded and upgraded.
* Water
  The water supply, managed by the Penang Water Authority, complies with the WHO standards for potable water. While the present capacity will meet the demand of the state up to the year 2000, two large new water schemes are presently being implemented.
* Telecommunications
  Telecommunication services in Penang are among the best and the most modern in the South-east Asian region. Penang has a penetration of 23 telephones per 100 population, compared to the national average of 10.

Industrial Parks

To initiate and facilitate the establishment of factories, particularly export-oriented factories, Penang pioneered Malaysia's first Free Industrial Zone (FIZ) or Export Processing Zone (EPZ) in 1972. To date, the state development agency, the Penang Development Corporation (PDC), has developed two FIZs and five industrial parks covering a total area of 5,850 acres (2,370 hectares).

The FIZs and the industrial parks provide ready sites for foreign MNCs and local support companies to set up factories within a short start-up time, usually less than a year. This is an important factor as MNCs need to "catch" the business cycle within a specific time frame to meet orders and to remain in business.

Institutional Framework

Much of the success in the industrialization process has been due to the efficient way the PDC has handled the industrialists for the last 25 years, since its inception in 1970 as the principal state development agency. The PDC prides itself in providing service to the industrialists from the first day of enquiry to well after the factories have been set up and operational. In fact, PDC strongly believes in good after-sales service and continues to be a good corporate friend of the investors.

The PDC hot line and even the Chief Minister's office are readily accessible and available when a problem is encountered or anticipated. From feedback received, the investors appreciate and value this commitment given by the state and the PDC. The PDC even acts as a catalyst to identify local joint-venture partners for foreign companies wishing to forge strategic alliances for purposes of local market penetration.

At the level of policy formulation and planning, the views of the investors and the private sector are sought. Active industry associations provide an effective sounding board and channel for investors' views to be heard.

Initiative and Ingenuity of the People

The people of Penang are by nature industrious and keen to learn. These qualities make adaptability to technological change much easier. Their excellent command of English and their eagerness to pursue new technologies have contributed to the fast development of the manufacturing and service sectors. This has resulted in the Penang operations of many MNCs being rated as among the best in their groups worldwide.

The small and medium scale industries (SMIs) operated by the local people played a very important role in Penang's industrial development. The local SMIs produce goods and services of the highest standards ranging from complete consumer goods to high tech sub-contracting work, fulfilling and satisfying the needs of the MNCs. Such a phenomenon has come about through 20 years of industrial development and technological transfer. In fact, the Penang SMIs are rated as quality vendors and have emerged as suppliers of world-class components and parts to disk drive, electronics and telecommunication industries.

Technical Training

Penang has always considered its people its most valuable asset and places great emphasis on education and training, in line with the needs of the economic and technological development of the state.

In the late 1980s when the state started to promote high technology industries, the PDC recognised the need to provide industry-specific technical training for the people. In line with the philosophy of "partners in progress", the PDC, with the cooperation of industry and academia, established the *Penang Skills Development Centre* (PSDC) in 1989.

The PSDC is a unique institution which pools the resources of the private sector, the government and academia to conduct technical training courses for operational skills as well as to keep abreast of technological progress. Supported by the government and managed by a committee drawn from the private sector, the PSDC, through its training laboratories, provides state-of-the-art training in technical skills, manufacturing skills, management skills and continuing education.

Arising from the success of the PSDC, Penang has set up two other industry-specific training centers, namely:

- the *Plastics Technology Centre* to conduct certificate-level courses in plastics technology. This center is run by the Malaysian Plastics Manufacturers Association and;
- the *Institute of Precision Molds* which is dedicated to training mold-making technicians, based on the curriculum of a leading Japanese polytechnic institution.

Penang will soon be home to the *Japan-Malaysia Technical Institute* (JMTI). This is a joint venture project by the Japanese and Malaysian governments and will offer engineering courses in mechatronics, instrumentation, control systems and production engineering.

International and Regional Cooperation

Penang is the second smallest state in Malaysia with a land area of 1,031 sq km and a population of 1.2 million. However Penang is not unknown to the rest of the world. Tourists call it the "Pearl of the Orient"; industrialists refer to Penang as the "Silicon Island of the East", a reference to the presence of many semiconductor and electronics factories.

Penang is small but it is reaching out and making its presence felt. As a small state with limited resources, Penang has to expand its hinterland by promoting regional cooperation .

Penang initiated regional cooperation with its neighboring states, and today there is a formal grouping known as the Northern States of Peninsular Malaysia, comprising the states of Perlis, Kedah (home state of Prime Minister Dr Mahathir), Penang (home state of Deputy Prime Minster and concurrently Finance Minister Anwar Ibrahim) and Perak (home state of International Trade and Industry

Minister Rafidah). This regional grouping has a total land area of 32,257 sq km and a population of 4.9 million.

On an international basis, Penang was instrumental in promoting the idea of a growth triangle with south Thailand and the northern part of the Indonesian Island of Sumatra. This concept of the Indonesia-Malaysia-Thailand Growth Triangle (IMT GT) was first promoted in 1990 to spur regional cooperation in economic activities and to accelerate development by making the best use of the advantages of each participating nation.

The IMT GT area with a combined population of 21 million and a host of resources, offers investors a variety of ways to exploit economic advantages within the region. For example, by shifting labor-intensive industries to neighboring Indonesia and Thailand, Penang can concentrate its energies in the field of technological development, as well as in research and development.

Penang has also developed a very extensive network through special arrangements with Kanagawa (Japan), Xiamen (China), Adelaide (Australia) and North Sumatra (Indonesia), as well as other international connections and relationships .

With its experience in manufacturing and services, Penang is poised to play a central and key role in this fast developing region of a borderless manufacturing society.

Future Directions

Penang has reached a stage of development where it is ready to move into new areas of higher technology. In fact, to remain competitive, Penang must be driven by productivity which in turn can be brought about through emphasis on technological upgrading, skills development, training and quality.

Various opportunities of investment exist in the fields of :

- Upstream electronics related to the semiconductor, hard disk drive, personal computer and telecommunications industry
- Advanced materials such as special polymers and plastics, formulation and compounding

- Automotive parts, mainly electrical and electronic, electro-mechanical components
- The aerospace industry, mainly electronic and electrical, electro-mechanical components, light aircraft
- Environmental engineering such as treatment of toxic waste, recycling industry

There are also opportunities for:

- Joint ventures in the electronic and computer components industry
- Research and development through the assembly of finished products in the field of turnkey manufacturing and marketing
- Development of pharmaceutical and chemical products, as well as joint research and development efforts with the School of Pharmacy at the local university.

Moving Forward

Penang has done well and has succeeded in transforming its economy from entrepot trade and agriculture to that based on the manufacturing sector. Within the manufacturing sector, Penang began with labor-intensive simple assembly-type industries. Building upon this base it moved on to technology-intensive, skill-intensive, knowledge-intensive industries.

Penang will not rest on its laurels but will move forward to prepare for the challenges of the 21st century. It will attempt to achieve the Malaysian Vision 2020 in a shorter period. It hopes to reach a "developed" state status in the year 2002.

To support and serve the manufacturing sector, Penang will emphasise the development and growth of its services sector, particularly in trade, logistics and transportation, educational services and medical services. Penang believes that all these are achievable with the support and cooperation of the private sector. The governmental framework will be strengthened to match the demands and requirements of the private sector. At the same time, the private sector is expected to be the main engine to drive this move forward towards a more prosperous 21st century. The final objective is to ensure a sustainable development effort, in harmony with the environment, for our future generations.

Chapter 6

China's Economic Growth: Challenges and Opportunities for Europe

Gregory C. Chow

In the first half of the 21st century world economic power will be shared by Europe, North America and Asia. Modern economic development began in Europe with the Industrial Revolution, followed by development in the United States and Canada, and more recently, in many Asian countries. The latest country to become an economic power is China. Because of its large population China's rise to an economic giant has a great impact on the balance of economic and political power in the world. Today I am honored to speak to this distinguished group of European and Asian leaders gathered in Switzerland on the nature of China's economic growth, the opportunities this presents for Europe and the challenges it poses.

Having been the leaders of the world for more than three centuries Europeans have witnessed with some apprehension the rise of the United States, especially during the Second World War, and more recently the rise of Asian countries including China. In the second half of the 20th century Europe lost its dominance to the United States and in the first half of the twenty-first century Europe and the United States will share their power with China, Japan and other Asian countries. We hope that later in the 21st century African and Latin American nations will experience rapid economic growth as well. World economic development and economic integration are good for all of us. Within a country people prefer a balanced growth with the increase in wealth shared by all citizens rather than being concentrated in the hands of a few. The same ideal applies to the economic development of nations. Furthermore, as Adam Smith pointed out in the *Wealth of Nations* (1776), division of labor and specialization lead to efficient economic production, and competition among individual productive units each pursuing its self interests in the market place will benefit the country as a whole. Similarly, division of labor and competition among nations are benefiting the world as a whole. Competition between China and European nations is inevitable as each country pursues its self interest. On the other hand trade and foreign investment have benefited both Europe and China. The question I would like to address is how we can improve on the economic relationship.

1. Nature of China's Economic Growth

To help improve economic relations between European countries and China, it is necessary to understand the nature of China's economy and its growth process. In the 1920's and 1930's, before the Sino-Japanese war beginning in 1937 and the civil war ending in 1949 when the People's Republic of China was founded, China's economy was essentially a market economy. Some 85 percent of the labor force was engaged in agriculture while some light industries were being developed in the coastal provinces. Economic development was hindered by the war with Japan and the civil war that followed. Peace in 1949 brought about recovery and growth until 1958 when Chairman Mao launched the Great Leap Forward movement to change the cooperative farms organized in the middle 1950's to Communes and to raise the output of steel by converting iron tools in backyard furnaces. The economy collapsed. It is estimated by demographer Ansley Coale that some 27 million people died during the Great Leap period from 1958 to 1963. Yum K. Kwan of the Hong Kong University of Science and Technology and I (1995) have estimated that if the Great Leap had not occurred per capita output in China in the early 1990's would have been about twice as large as the actual amount. After some economic recovery following the Great Leap Mao started the Cultural Revolution of 1965–1975. Human suffering and the loss of morality was great during those 10 years but the economic loss (narrowly defined as the loss of physical output measured by official statistics) was much less than during the Great Leap. Without the Cultural Revolution, China's real national output per capita would have been about 1.2 times its historical figure in the early 1990's. In spite of the great suffering inflicted upon the Chinese people, Premier Zhao Ziyang once said to me in 1985, the Cultural Revolution had the positive effect of freeing the Chinese people from a restrictive ideology.

China adopted Soviet-style central economic planning in 1953 with the first Five-Year Plan that year. It is beginning its ninth Five-Year Plan in 1996 (as it started its third Plan in 1966 after an adjustment period following the Great Leap). Although the extent of central economic planning was limited and varied according to political circumstances from 1953 to 1978 when economic reform began, much of the market economy that had existed in 1949 was destroyed. Private farming was replaced by collective farming by large teams of farmers in the Communes. Trade of agricultural and other rural products was replaced by compulsory purchase by government agencies. Private industrial enterprises were abolished or transformed to state, provincial or local enterprises. Even peddlers, small shops, private raising of pigs and chickens in Communes, and rural markets were prohibited during the Cultural Revolution as being capitalistic. When Deng Xiaoping started economic reforms in 1978 the country was ready for a change. The new leaders could dissociate themselves from the mistakes of Mao. Officials in the government had learned from sad experience the economic inefficiency of central economic planning. Furthermore, the successful economic development of Taiwan, which was achieved by adopting a market economy provided the needed stimulus and example. The farmers knew only too well the advantages of private farming as compared with the Commune system. The responsible system, which assigned a piece of land to each farm family and collected from it a fixed amount of produce (rent) while allowing it to reap all the profits from the sales of its output in the market was initiated by local Commune leaders. When the system was demonstrated to have resulted in large increases in output, the central government adopted it as a national policy in 1979. This was the center piece at the beginning of China's economic reform. It was successful, as compared with the agricultural reform in Russia, partly because Chinese farmers in 1978 still knew private farming, having been prohibited from doing it only in 1958 and allowed to return to it partially during the recovery of 1963–65.

Having succeeded in reforming its agriculture China began its urban and industrial reform in the early 1980's. The policy was not to privatize the state enterprises but to change the rules of their operations to make them more efficient. China continued to be a socialist country with due emphasis on the role of the state enterprises. However, the enterprises were given autonomy to make decisions concerning the production of their outputs, the acquisition of their inputs, the marketing of their products and the investment of their retained earnings. Limited autonomy was first introduced to some six thousand state enterprises. After successful experimental results were observed a higher degree of autonomy was extended to more enterprises. In 1987 a contract responsibility system was introduced to almost all state enterprises. Under this system state enterprises were allowed to keep all the profits after surrendering a supposedly fixed amount of annual tax to the government unit controlling them for a period of five years. In October 1984 an important decision of the Central Committee of the Chinese Communist Party was passed to provide guidelines for further reform. It consisted of seven elements: (1) more autonomy for state enterprises, (2) a change from mandatory planning to guidance planning, (3) allowing more prices to be decontrolled, (4) developing macroeconomic control mechanisms together with an improved financial and banking system, (5) introducing responsibility systems for units within enterprises to promote efficiency, (6) fostering the development of individual and collective enterprises as a supplement to state enterprises, (7) expanding foreign trade and investment and technological exchanges. Today the most successful records are in (6) and (7), and the least are (1) and (4). Thus while collective and individual enterprises as well as foreign and jointly operated enterprises provide dynamic growth to compensate for the slow growth of state enterprises, modern macroeconomic control mechanisms and a modern banking system are yet to be established in China.

As economic reforms were gradually introduced much of the energy and ingenuity of Chinese workers and entrepreneurs were being released to develop the Chinese economy. The rate of growth of real material output in China from 1979 to 1995 averaged over 9.5 percent per year, with higher than average growth occurring in 1992–1995. Over 70 percent of the output of China, including almost all of agriculture and some 60 percent of industry, is produced by economic units for profit as in a market economy. The market component of China's production and distribution system is large enough to sustain rapid growth of, say, over eight percent per year for at least two more decades, as I see nothing in the foreseeable future to hinder the continued growth except for an unlikely and yet unpredictable political turmoil. China will therefore be a larger economic power to contend with in the first half of the twenty-first Century.

2. Competition from China

Economic competition from China has come and will intensify in the coming decades As pointed out in my introduction and as we have witnessed, competition among nations is good for the world. If competition between General Motors, Ford and Chrysler are good for America, why is competition between Italy, Taiwan and the United States not good for the world? Of course each company or nation subject to competitive pressure has to work hard to survive and the people employed in sectors adversely affected may have to seek alternative employment, but this is a fact of life that Europeans and Asians have to accept. Toynbee has suggested that some stimulus from outside is good for a civilization, and such a stimulus is coming for both Europeans and Asians.

In what ways are the Chinese competitive? First, China has a vast and high-quality labor force, with much of the high quality derived from an old culture of good handicrafts, respect for intellectual pursuits and the habit of working hard. Chinese are skillful in making electronic products; Chinese are good computer programmers and designers of computer software. Also, Chinese labor is cheap at all skill levels. Second, Chinese are good merchants and entrepreneurs, as demonstrated by their performance in Hong Kong, Taiwan and South-east Asia. Third, China has adopted an open-door policy that allows investment and technology to flow in from economically more advanced countries and especially from overseas Chinese. As a result we have found many foreign joint ventures in China utilizing the cheap and skillful labor force to produce goods for exports to the world market. China produced for the world market processed food, sports goods, watches, clothing, electronics and almost any manufactured goods except automobiles and computers. According to official Chinese custom statistics (see *Statistical Yearbook of China 1993*, p. 633 and 1994, pp. 512–514), the volume of Chinese foreign trade in U.S. dollars grew at an annual rate of nearly 20 percent in the first half of the 1990's. China's export in 1993 amounted to $91.8 billion U.S. and its imports amounted to $104 billion. Asia accounted for $52.6 billion of China's export and $63 billion of China's import. Europeans purchased $16.4 billion of China's exports and provided $24.0 billion of China's imports. The United States purchased $17.0 billion exports from China and shipped $10.7 billion imports to China. Thus while the U.S. is running a trade deficit with China, Europe is having a trade surplus with China. In the future China will be able to compete in technologically more advanced manufactured goods as well as financial services, especially after Hong Kong is returned to China in 1997. What are the opportunities resulting from China's economic growth?

3. Opportunities for Europeans

A. Profit-Making Opportunities

Let me first discuss the profit-making opportunities. By producing what is needed in China, either demanded by the governments at different levels or by the consumers, and by producing in China for exports an European company can make profits. The Chinese government is eager to build infrastructure including highways, ports, telecommunication systems, etc. that require modern technology which China does not have. Chinese state enterprises are also looking for foreign partners to upgrade its technology, management, labor and marketing abilities. These needs are well known. Many Europeans have already been taking advantage of them. The Chinese consumer markets are being open wider as import quotas and tariffs are being reduced, partly as a result of the Chinese government's desire to join APEC and WTO and partly as a result of the rapid increase in China's reserve of hard currencies which can be spent to increase imports. Besides selling to the Chinese market European companies can also take advantage of the cheap and skilled labor in China to produce for exports and many companies have done so already. To take advantage of economic opportunities in China Europeans may find the following suggestions useful.

(1) *Finding the right contacts*

Doing business in China is different from doing business in Western countries mainly because in China economic power is to a large extent in the hands of bureaucracies at different levels of government, because China does not have a Western-style legal system and because Chinese workers and managers have different habits, ethics, outlooks and training from those found in the West. To do business one needs approval and help from the Chinese bureaucracies, in addition to assistance from Chinese labor and management. To set up a business or joint venture you need the approval of many levels of the government, possibly including the central government in Beijing, a provincial and/or local government, ministry A and/or bureau (a) as well as ministry B and/or bureau (b), etc. It sounds like an impossible task. In each step, the approval or required agreement may take a long time and require patient negotiations. Many Western companies have had the sad experience of believing that the agreement of one or two Chinese bureaucrats is sufficient to conduct its business, only to find that many more bureaucrats must grant approval or at least must be dealt with. Some less relevant bureaus or people can simply give you trouble in order to reap some profits from your operations. The reason for the existence of so many bureaucrats surrounding your project is that almost all bureaucrats are looking constantly at opportunities to make money in the same way that all Western business men are looking for opportunities to make money. They are working under a system in which economic power is still in the hands of the government bureaucracy to a large extent.

Now that you are all given a warning, what can I suggest for you to find the right contact? Your contact or partner must have the authority, or be able to acquire sufficient authority, to do the business desired. If the person or the agency is the right one, he/she can get the approval, or can help you get the approval from all others that may be trying to extract something from you. If you cannot find such a person you should not do business in China. How do you find such a person? That depends partly on what your business is and how much you have to offer. If you have a world recognized product to sell that China needs, the task is easy because many Chinese bureaucrats would be chasing after you and you only need to pick the right partner among them. Choosing the right person requires your ability to recognize who knows what. If you have such an ability, by definition, you can find the right people. Otherwise you cannot.

(2) *Be patient in negotiations*

This suggestion is obvious in view of the discussion on the last point. It is strengthened by the point that follows. I make this point of the need to be patient explicit so that you can plan your project accordingly. You have to figure in the extra time in your cost calculation and time allocation. It is not unusual for the negotiation to complete a contract for a joint venture to take more than two years, depending on your skill, experience and knowledge of China and the Chinese.

(3) *Accept the semi-legal framework*

Many Western businessmen and scholars complain that there is an absence of a Western style legal system in China and therefore it is hard to do business in China. Whether one complains about it or not, it is a fact that one has to live with if one wants to do business in China. As an economist I am much interested in the questions as to why such a non-legal system (in the Western sense) has flourished in China and whether and in what way it is better or worse than the Western legal system. Suffice it to state here that such a non-legal system has functioned in China for a long time and it has worked, although some Westerners do not like the way it works while some Chinese might think it is a superior system. Whatever your opinion is, to do business in China you cannot depend too much on the current system of Chinese law, which is recognized to be imperfect by both Westerners and Chinese. You will increase your profits by accepting the existing imperfect Chinese legal system and learning to do business the Chinese way. By that I mean you have to develop a network in China, getting to know the right people and making the right friends. This is called developing *Guanxi* in Chinese. Interpreted in modern economic terms Guanxi is a kind of human capital both in the sense of your knowing and having access to influential people in China and their recognition that you are useful to them. Establishing personal connections in order to do business better is common in Western societies, but the degree to which you have to rely on it as compared with the formal legal system is much higher in China. Accepting this fact alone will help you to conduct business successfully in China. Note, however, that the way to befriend Chinese may be somewhat different and you have to know some Chinese customs. A very simple issue is who pays the bill when two good friends go out to eat. By the Western way each pays his/her own bill. By the Chinese way only one person pays the bill. When a Westerner sees his friend pay he may smile and feel that he is getting something free. When a Chinese sees the same he would often prefer to have paid the bill himself because it is an honor to pay and perhaps his friend feels indebted to him, so that in the future his friend will do something for him if he needs it. Being a host is like putting money in the bank which you can draw on in the future when you need it.

If you cannot depend on legal contracts how can you be sure that your partner will keep his part of the bargain? The way to insure it is to remain useful to him or to stay in a position such that he will depend on you in the future. If you have a contract to share profits in the future how do you guarantee that your Chinese partner will honor the contract? When Mr. Roebuck presumably lost his usefulness to Mr. Sears, the company's name is changed from Sears-Roebuck to Sears. This can also happen in China. To maintain your usefulness you have to keep your other business connections and maintain your influence in the world business community so that your Chinese partner will continue to value a good relation with you. If I were speaking to a Chinese audience on how to maintain a good relation with Western partners, I would say the same thing — try to maintain your position in the business community so that your Western partner will keep his promises to you or will keep his partnership with you in the future rather than with someone else. If you lose your usefulness as a partner almost no legal protection can keep the partnership for you. It is wise for a potential investor in China to adapt to the Chinese semi-legal system. However, from a historical perspective, China's legal system is going to improve in the next century as the system has already improved a great deal in the last 15 years because of the need to deal with foreign investors.

(4) *Technology transfer to China*

Somewhat related to the fact of an imperfect legal system in China is the lack of sufficient protection of patents and copyrights in China. This issue has been discussed in the Western press. Within the informal framework of doing business what prevents a Chinese partner, who is producing some products in a joint venture with you, from setting up a separate factory using the technology which you have introduced? Without sufficient legal protection you can hardly stop your Chinese partner from doing so. Western investors are aware of this and have tried to devise means to protect their interests, for example, by keeping an essential part of the technology secret and known to only a limited number of people whom they can trust. If some technology or patent is difficult to protect from a technical point of view the investor has to take this fact into account when investing in China, possibly by reaping enough profits in a short time before the technology can be copied or by sacrificing a calculated part of the Chinese market while maintaining a large part of the international market which is protected legally. Even protection in international markets can be uncertain as recent newspapers are full of stories of Chinese manufacturers copying video tapes, compact discs, movies and software packages for export into the international market. The number of pirated products in China offered for sale in the world market is so large as to draw much attention in the world community.

There is no solution yet for the problem of pirating in China. This phenomenon is easy to understand from the historical and cultural background of the Chinese. Patents are a recent product of world history after the Industrial Revolution. There were not too many scientific inventions to protect in Chinese history. If the Chinese knew of a certain way to produce useful drugs, for example, they would keep it a family secret. Many products in China were protected in this way. If products cannot be so protected they are generally available, including all the herbs that are sold in traditional Chinese drugstores and are therefore available to benefit the Chinese population. The lack of patent protection is said to be bad for the society because it may discourage people from inventing new products. The possible harm of patents is to close the market for potential inventors of related products which might infringe on patent rights. Also, without patents the new products would be available to consumers at lower prices. Before legal protection can be effectively enforced in China, foreign businessmen and governments have to accept this fact. In February 1996 the United States government registered a strong protest to the Government in Beijing against the large number of Chinese pirated products being marketed. This worsened the already tense diplomatic relations between the two countries. This protest had the same effect as would a protest to the government of Mexico that illegal drugs from Mexico were sold in America. The difference is that some of the Chinese products were said to be produced by firms which are otherwise legal in China, in some cases allegedly firms affiliated with the Chinese military. The similarity is that in both cases there is simply so much money to be made that the two governments have found it difficult to stop the illegal activity, marking such a protest only mildly effective.

(5) *Cooperation with Chinese state enterprises*

There are a number of examples of successful joint ventures between a foreign investor and a Chinese state enterprise controlled by the central, provincial or local government. By successful I mean both the Chinese and the foreign partners have made money. Such joint ventures are still available and plentiful if the foreign investor is wise enough to find them. The advantage of helping to operate a state enterprise is that the Chinese partner is likely to have sufficient authority to produce and market the product and may even have sufficient power to protect the product from infringement by piracy. If the foreign investor can find ways to protect his share of the profits, as discussed above, there may be much profit to be made by both partners. A potential investor should study the successful cases to find out what makes the cooperation successful. He or she should also look into successful cases of cooperation with township and village enterprises. These enterprises, in contrast with the slow growing state enterprises, constitute a very important component of the rapid economic growth of China.

B. Nonprofit Cooperation with the Chinese

Forum Engelberg has a number of participants who are interested in technology transfer to and technological cooperation with China to benefit the world. Some of these activities are not, or not mainly, profit motivated. For example Cornell University in the United States is currently interested in cooperating with appropriate people in China to transfer its knowledge of agricultural technology to China. Whatever its motivations, Cornell has developed technologies in many fields which have benefited mankind. Several of the points made above to insure successful cooperation with the Chinese are valid here. One has to find the right partner, be patient in negotiations with the Chinese, accept the fact that things get done by personal connections and influence, and to deal with Chinese technological, scientific or educational institutions which have authority and power in the area of work that they do. Finding the right people in the right organization to cooperate with is the most important factor of guaranteeing success. I have cooperated with Chinese organizations to promote economic education and economic reform in China. In both cases I was fortunate to find the right people in the right organizations, these being the State Education Commission and the State Commission for Restructuring the Economic System respectively. The results of over 10 years of cooperation with the first Commission and over four years with the second have been successful and gratifying. The experience is recorded in Chapter 5 of my book *Understanding China's Economy* (World Scientific, 1994).

My experience is that China is full of well-meaning, trustworthy and very talented people. Of course China has its share of corrupt officials, as we have found in many other countries, East and West. If we can find the right people to cooperate with in pursuing our common objectives we can be very successful. The right people are not difficult to find. After 17 years of open-door policy China's talented and trustworthy people are known to the world or at least to other Chinese who are known to the world. Through direct or indirect contact with people one knows, a European entrepreneur, scientist or educator can find the right people in the right Chinese organizations to cooperate with. In spite of the recent military maneuver around the Taiwan Strait a serious military conflict between Mainland China and Taiwan is unlikely as neither side has anything to gain by such an engagement. I am optimistic about future economic cooperation between Europe and China. May I wish all of you success in cooperating with people in China to build a happier and more prosperous world community in the 21st century.

Acknowledgments

The author would like to thank Joseph I. Coffey and Michael Bordo for helpful comments on an early draft of this paper.

References

CHOW, G. C., 1985, *The Chinese Economy*, 2nd edition, Singapore: World Scientific

________, 1994, *Understanding China's Economy*, Singapore: World Scientific

KWAN, Y. K. and G. C. Chow, 1995, Estimating Economic Effects of Political Movements in China. Princeton University Econometric Research Program Research Memorandum #372

SMITH, A., 1776, *Wealth of Nations*, New York, N.Y.: The Modern Library, 1937 edition

Statistical Yearbook of China 1993. State Statistics Bureau, Beijing

Statistical Yearbook of China 1994. State Statistics Bureau, Beijing

PART II

SOCIO-POLITICAL ISSUES

Chapter 7

Human Rights in China and the Future of Hong Kong

John Kamm

It is a pleasure to be back in Hong Kong, which for 23 years — from 1972 to 1995 — was my home. I returned with my family to the United States in July last year. I have two young boys, ages nine and five, and I very much wanted them to spend a good part of their formative years growing up in the country of which they are citizens, the United States. Though I have very fond memories of Hong Kong — and I continue to maintain an office and a residence here — I have no regrets at all about the decision I made.

Young boys bring with them many blessings and also all kinds of problems. My father was a whiskey salesman, and while I dabble in the area of human rights, by profession I'm a chemical salesman. I guess you'd say I have sales in the blood. The folks I hang around with in the chemical industry and in "the oil patch" are very fond of telling jokes, and my two boys love jokes. Unfortunately, most of the jokes I hear are not the kind which can be readily told to nine and five year-olds, especially nine and five year-olds who go to Catholic schools. I was recently told a joke, however, that my boys like very much, and since it brings to mind one of the reasons I came to the Far East a quarter century ago, it bears telling here.

It seems that there was a mother mouse who was showing her three little ones around their new dwelling. She showed them the good places to hide, to play, to store food. As she was turning a corner with the little ones close behind she found herself face-to-face with a big, ferocious cat. The mommy mouse reared up on her back legs, assuming the fullest height she could, and, looking the cat square in the eyes she said "Woof, woof!" The startled cat took fright and scampered away, whereupon the mommy mouse turned to her little ones and said "Now my dears, you see the value of a second language."

It was my mother who convinced me to take Chinese at Princeton, and I was fortunate that Princeton's Chinese teachers were then and are today the best in America. My mother told me, in the summer of 1969 after I had just graduated from a troubled urban high school, that if you know a somewhat exotic language you'll always be able to find a job. In 1972, after taking three years of Chinese, I graduated from Princeton and headed out to Macau for a teaching job arranged through Princeton-in-Asia, an organization that has placed so many young people in positions where they can influence — and be influenced by — Asians. My timing was excellent. In 1972, President Nixon made his historic visit to China. I have witnessed and occasionally played a small role in the process of China's opening up to the outside world, a process which can, in many respects, be dated to the historic opening engineered by Nixon and Kissinger the year I graduated from Princeton.

I am now known mostly for my work in human rights. From time to time I make trips to Beijing and discuss this very sensitive subject with officials of the Chinese government. I have probably worked on the cases of more than 300 individuals imprisoned for political reasons. Given this experience, and in light of the critical remarks I've made on many occasions about the Chinese government's record in the area of human rights, what I am about to say might strike you as strange, even incongruous. Those of us who witnessed what China was like 20 or 25 years ago, during the waning days of the Cultural Revolution, know that there has been very considerable progress in the area of human rights since then. When one has witnessed the hell that was China in those days, we, Americans and others who live in open, Democratic societies, can appreciate how truly fortunate we are and indeed how fortunate the people of China are to have had leaders brave enough to embark upon what has been a great experiment.

In the remarks that follow I will not mince words. I will not trivialize the very serious abuses of human rights going on in China. But unless you put the criticism of China's current human rights situation against the backdrop of the way things were, and appreciate the achievements that have been made, then today's critique cannot be understood or acted on in a responsible way. In responding to a criticism directed at Martin Luther King, Jr.'s nonviolent philosophy by the author James Baldwin, the theologian Reinhold Niebuhr said that "The great ethical divide is between people who want to be pure and people who want to be responsible." The choice for Americans confronting the challenge of what to do about human rights violations in China is precisely the choice between being pure and being responsible.

What was it like to live in Mao's China? It was a society that was totalitarian in the extreme. The cult of personality pervaded every aspect of life. We speak today of "civil society" — that set of institutions outside of government or party control that binds individuals together into communities. Civil society disappeared in Mao's China. There was no system of justice. China was a vast police state, egalitarian in a radical way. If someone were perceived to be a member of — or the relative of a member of — a reactionary class, or even if he or she were seen as somehow "different", he or she and the members of his or her family suffered grievously.

Dissent was not tolerated at all. The first Democracy Movement in post-1949 China began in Guangzhou in 1974. It started with a wall poster calling for socialist democracy and law. The post was put up by three young workers — Li Jengtian, Chen Yiyang and Wang Xizhe — and the group they led was known by the acronym Li Yizhe, formed by taking a syllable from each of their names. I had only been living in Hong Kong for a couple of years when the Li Yizhe movement began. China was closed then, and I knew of Li Yizhe only through press accounts in Hong Kong. Little did

I know that, 20 years later, I'd become involved in the lives of these men.

Mao was still alive when Li Yizhe put up their wall poster. In those days in China, the government response to such an incident was to immediately arrest those responsible, and if it was deemed to be a serious counter-revolutionary incident, those arrested would be executed. Today in China people are sentenced to prison for counter-revolutionary incitement and propaganda, but in those days they were executed.

Those of you who have seen the film *Schindler's List* might recall a particularly powerful scene in which Schindler convinces the camp commandant, for a brief period, that real power - the power of the Caesars — was the power to forgive and be merciful. Mao, already in the last years of his life, for some unexplained reason decided that — instead of immediately executing this group of dissidents — the party ideologues would have to defeat them first in debate.

The Central Committee assembled a team of Marxist-Leninist-Mao Tse-tung Thought philosophers and the three workers were "struggled" for more than 100 sessions. Through deft manipulation of the party line, the dissidents time and again defeated the group from Party Central in Beijing. Mao ordained that, so long as the three remained undefeated in debate, they could not be put in prison or executed. Mao died in 1976, and the three were immediately thrown in jail. When they emerged, in 1979, one of them wrote an essay in which he told another famous story of "leniency". A woman in northeast China, in a dream shouted out "Down with Chairman Mao". This was most certainly an executable offense, but it was decided to take mercy on this woman and instead her tongue was cut out. This was how dissent was dealt with in Mao's China.

Let's look at China today. Let's look at Guangzhou, home of the Li Yizhe movement. Gone is the cult of personality we saw in the Mao years. There are minor cults of personality, like the one being built around Deng Xiaoping, but nothing even remotely of the scale of the Mao cult. There is a rudimentary system of justice.

In the China of Mao, we had rule by man. Now we have rule by law, not rule of law. Laws are used to carry out the decisions of the party. Hopefully, we will someday see rule of law in China. China is today an authoritarian as opposed to a totalitarian state. Contact with the outside world can still be a bit of a gamble, but compared with 20 years ago, when Chinese simply could not leave the country or even their home areas and travel to others, the situation has shown improvement. In the United States alone there are close to 50,000 Chinese students in the universities and colleges.

There are a great many problems in China today. There are growing disparities in income between different parts of the country, and this is giving rise to tension. Reliable reports of widespread violations of human rights have been made. The arbitrary powers of the police are still far too strong. Independent religious organizations don't exist. There is an underground Roman Catholic Church that recognizes the authority of the Pope in Rome and an officially-sponsored Catholic Church that doesn't recognize the Pope's supremacy. Yet again, if you compare it to 20 years ago, there is a measure of religious freedom and government tolerance.

This brings me to my last point. While there have been tremendous improvements in the living conditions and individual rights of the average Chinese, there is nevertheless a great gap between what we have here in Hong Kong and what we see in China. We are about to witness a merger between Hong Kong and China. Promises have repeatedly been made that the systems in place in Hong Kong won't change, but I think we have all come to realize that this is simply not realistic. Changes will take place; changes are already taking place.

Take for example the stipulation in the Basic Law that the legislature of the Hong Kong Special Administrative Region must pass laws against subversion. There is no law against subversion in the legal system currently in force in Hong Kong. There is no concept of subversion in the Common Law. What is it? Hong Kong must now come up with a law that prohibits acts of subversion against China. People cannot ignore the fact that Wei Jingsheng has just been sentenced to 14 years in prison for trying to subvert the Chinese government.

There is the very serious problem of the provisional Legislative Council. We face the problem of the application of International Human Rights Law in Hong Kong after 1997. The Basic Law stipulates that the provisions of the International Covenants on Human Rights in force before 1997 shall continue to apply after 1997. But how can this be achieved if the sovereign country — China — is not itself a signatory to those covenants?

I share with Gordon Wu the brave optimism that has somehow always characterized this place called Hong Kong. Its survival in the face of all odds is truly a miraculous story. It probably would have been best for all concerned if the merger could have been put off for a few more years. That alas, is not to be. As long as this place can continue to enjoy the presence and the leadership of men like Gordon Wu, a man not afraid to put his money where his mouth is — which Princeton has learned to its very considerable benefit — then there is hope that the Hong Kong people can overcome the very serious difficulties arising from the transition of a free, capitalist society to a territory under the control of the world's last communist state, China.

Thank you.

Chapter 8

Singapore's Economic and Social Development

Richard Eu

I will be focusing my talk on the developments in Singapore for the past three decades, dealing largely with the areas of economic, social and political development, and the country's competitive position in the world.

Real GDP Growth and Inflation

Singapore's economy posted an average real GDP growth rate of 8.5 percent between 1960 and 1994.

Table 1: Gross Domestic Product

Year	Growth in GDP (in percent)
1960–1964	5.5
1965–1973	12.0
1974–1984	7.8
1985–1986	0.15
1987–1994	9.0
1960–1994	8.5

Our steady economic progress has earned us the status of an advanced developing country. Its GDP per capita, which rose from $1,329 in 1960 to $31,181 in 1994, is higher than some industrial market economies of Spain, Ireland and Italy.

Table 2: Per Capita GNP

Year	GNP per capita ($)
1960	1,329.6
1970	2,825.3
1980	9.940.6
1990	22.587.4
1994	31.191.7

We are fortunate that this high GDP growth is accompanied by relative price stability, with a modest average inflation rate of 3.4 percent throughout the period.

Table 3: Inflation Rate

Year	Inflation (%)
1960–1969	1.2
1970–1979	5.6
1980–1989	3.9
1990–1994	2.9

Table 4: Balance of Payment

Year	Balance of payment ($m)
1960	140.1
1970	564.8
1980	1,433.8
1990	9,892.5
1994	7,302.0

Balance of Payment

While the nation registers a chronic deficit in trade and merchandise, this deficit is more than covered by surpluses in services. In fact, Singapore enjoys a healthy balance of payment every year since 1966. In 1994, the balance of payment surplus stood at $7,302 million.

Savings and Investments

It is a well-known fact that Singapore's national savings rate is among the highest in the world. The ratio of gross national savings to GNP has risen from a negative rate of −2.6 percent in 1960 to 49.7 percent in 1994.

Table 5: Gross National Savings (GNS)

Year	GNS as a % of GNP
1960	–2.6
1970	19.3
1980	34.7
1990	43.9
1994	49.7

This high rate of savings is attributable to both voluntary and compulsory private savings, as well as government savings.

In terms of investments, the nation's political stability and excellent infrastructure, including telecommunications networks, have helped significantly to attract funds. The rate of investment, as measured by the ratio of Gross Fixed Capital Formation to GNP, rose from a meager 9.4 percent in 1960 to a healthy 69.5 percent in 1994. A significant proportion of this increase came from foreign investments. For example in 1994, 75 percent of the $5.7 billion increase in net investments commitments in manufacturing were contributed by foreign investors.

Public Debt

With our large domestic savings, government's foreign borrowing is kept at a minimal level. Indeed, the public sector's external debt has been declining.

Table 6: External Public Debt

Year	External public debt ($m)	% of GNP
1970	173.8	3.0
1980	937.0	3.9
1990	67.9	0.1
1994	4.7	0.01

In 1994, it stood at $4.7 million, or 0.01 percent of GNP, compared with $173.8 million or 3 percent of GNP in 1970.

Social Indicators

Employment

I would now like to move on to cover the social developments of Singapore. The strengthening of Singapore's economy has translated into several social benefits. For example, the nation's unemployment rate fell from 8.9 percent in 1966 to 2.6 percent in 1994.

Table 7: Labor Force[1] and Unemployment Rate

Year	Labor force (in '000)	Unemployment rate (%)
1970	705	6.0
1980	1,093	3.6
1990	1,563	1.7
1994	1,693	2.6

[1] Labor Force refers to population aged 15 years and over who are employed as well as those unemployed but actively looking for a job.

As a matter of fact, since 1978 the Singapore economy has been experiencing a tight labor market. Alongside this development, we are seeing greater female participation rate which was 50.9 percent in 1994 compared with 22 percent in 1960.

Table 8: Sources of Labor Force Supply

Year	Total (%)	Female (%)	Male (%)	Share of non-Singaporeans in labor force (%)
1970	56.6	29.7	84.2	11.5
1980	63.4	47.2	84.7	6.2
1990	66.0	53.0	79.0	15.0
1994	64.9	50.9	79.6	21.0

Education

Accompanying the steady economic growth was an increase in the overall education of the workforce. The proportion of the workforce with post-secondary and higher qualifications has increased from 16.3 percent in 1985 to 26.6 percent in 1994.

Table 9: Educational Level of Labor Force

Year	Below secondary (%)	Secondary (%)	Post-secondary (%)
1985	54.5	29.2	16.3
1990	43.2	30.2	26.6

Gross Monthly Income

In line with the improvement in the educational qualifications of the work force, there has been a significant increase in workers' earnings. For instance, the proportion of employed persons earning less than $600 declined significantly from 60 percent in 1980 to 15.2 percent in 1994. Those who earned $1,500 and above rose from around 7.6 percent to 37.4 percent over the same period.

Table 10: Employed Persons by Gross Monthly Income

Year	Persons earning various levels of income (%)		
	< $600	$600–$1,500	> $1,500
1980	60	32.4	7.6
1994	15.2	47.4	37.4

Housing

Along with higher income, Singaporeans have also been benefiting from the housing projects undertaken by the Government. Some 86 percent of the population are housed in public flats, of which 80 percent are owner-occupied flats. This compares well with only 42 percent in 1980.

Table 11: Housing

Year	% of population living in public flats	% of population owning public flats
1960	9	—
1980	73	42
1990	87	80
1994	86	80

Challenges Posed by Low Population Growth and Change in Leaders

While we are enjoying healthy economic growth, the nation is experiencing persistently low fertility and mortality rates.

These continuing trends will likely to result in an aging population that will put a strain on the economy in terms of social security.

Politically, Singapore has just undergone a transfer of power to the second generation leaders led by Prime Minister Goh Chok Tong. A crucial component of this change was the establishment of team-rule in place of the one-man-rule of the first generation

Table 12: Population

Year	Population (million)	Rate of growth (%)
1960	1.6331	3.5
1970	2.0745	1.7
1980	2.4139	1.3
1990	2.7051	2.2
1994	2.9302	2.0

Table 13: Median Age, Dependency Ratio[2] and Index of Aging[3]

Year	Median age	Dependency ratio (%)	Index of aging (%)
1980	24.5	46.6	31.7
1990	29.8	47.7	39.4
1994	31.4	48.7	42.2

leaders. How the government and its people respond to these challenges will, in no small measure, affect Singapore's competitiveness in the world.

Political Developments

On 28 November 1990, Goh Chok Tong took over as Prime Minister of Singapore from Lee Kuan Yew who had held that office for more than 3 decades. This represented the transfer of power to the second generation leaders, chosen and trained as their successors by the first generation founding fathers of Singapore. Underlying the special importance he places on team rule, Mr Goh in May 1991, soon after taking over as Prime Minister stated:

[2] Residents under 15 years and those 60 years and over divided by residents aged 15–59 years.

[3] Residents aged 60 years and over divided by those under 15 years.

> "What we need is a team. As I have always said, Lee Kuan Yew is a one-man army, he's the sniper, he's the pilot, he's the driver, he's everything, he's all rolled in one. ... Our team has got to be rounded. No single person may be rounded as Mr Lee, but the team as a whole can be."

The political leadership and governing bureaucrats have become increasingly preoccupied with pro-active planning to meet the challenges of a maturing economy. Since the late 1980s, the PAP government has engaged in long-range strategic planning to prepare Singapore for the next stage of economic development. First and foremost, the government released a political manifesto, called *The Next Lap*, which offered in some detail the vision of the political leadership for the socio-economic, political and cultural development of the republic to enable it to join the league of industrialized nations.

To elaborate on the specific economic tasks to achieve the vision of *The Next Lap*, the government economic planners embarked on a strategic economic planning exercise in 1989, culminating in the release of a Strategic Economic Plan (SEP) for Singapore in 1991 that outlines the specific thrusts for economic development over the next decade (see Appendix A).

Besides the SEP, which covers the economy as a whole, the government has also released a number of sector-specific plans for economic development in the 1990s. These include

a) a New Technology Plan (NTP) to spearhead Singapore's drive towards a technological innovation, and research and development-driven industrialization;
b) a new information technology development masterplan, called IT2000, to prepare the information infrastructures for the 21st Century; and
c) other plans such as the Automation Masterplan, and an SME Masterplan;
d) a Land Transport Authority's New Paper.

Even more recently, Prime Minister Goh Chok Tong has stressed the need for the development of a gracious society. He has also indicated that even at this moment, the second generation political leaders are on the lookout for the third generation political leaders to be in place in the year 2020.

World Competitive Report

In the 1994 World Competitive Report, Singapore, in spite of the constraints linked to its size and lack of natural resources, was ranked second overall. It ranked first in the government and the people factors, two very valuable long-term assets for the future of Singapore.

An important finding to take note of is that Singapore ranked only seventh for management, with a modest 24th ranking for the sub-factor of entrepreneurship. Its performance in terms of science and technology was also modest, securing an eighth rank, with weak performance in the sub-factor of research and technology which was ranked in the 20th position.

Even though Singapore ranked first in terms of education system overall, we only ranked 22nd in terms of public expenditure on education per capita. Interestingly, we ranked as one of the lowest among the NIEs for this particular factor, below Taiwan and Hong Kong. Another area for improvement is female participation in the work force, which was ranked 27th. Given the shortage of workers in Singapore, more can be done to increase the female participation rate.

The report also highlighted that while the Singapore work force's attitude came out top, the sub-factor of willingness to retrain only managed a ranking of seven.

Thus, although Singapore's overall performance according to the Report is encouraging, there are areas which need attention. Many developing countries are no doubt increasing their efforts to sharpen their competitive edge. For Singapore to remain competitive, we need to strengthen our position in the weaker areas that I have mentioned.

Conclusion

While we may bask in our nation's success, an honest recognition of our weaknesses and the willingness to put forth efforts to improve is, I believe, the only appropriate response to the Report.

I do not think that this is a very tall order for Singapore. Although it lacks a natural resource base, this fact has been the underlying factor in the country's planning, and the Government has so far managed to come out resilient and strong. Like most Singaporeans, I have confidence in the Government, and especially in the people.

APPENDIX A

Thrusts of Singapore's Strategic Economic Plan (SEP)

Strategic Thrust 1	**Enhancing Human Resources**
Program 1	International Manpower Program
Strategic Thrust 2	**Promoting National Teamwork**
Program 2	Establishment of an Economic Panel
Strategic Thrust 3	**Becoming Internationally Oriented**
Program 3	Preparing Singaporeans for International Assignments
Program 4	Promoting the Growth Triangle and Alliance with the Region
Program 5	Developing Information Infrastructure
Strategic Thrust 4	**Creating a Conducive Climate for Innovation**
Program 6	Reviewing Government Rules which Hinder Innovation

Strategic Thrust 5	**Developing Manufacturing and Service Clusters**
Program 7	Implementation of Cluster-based Development Plans
Program 8	Cluster Workshops
Program 9	Improving the Bond between Employees and Employers
Program 10	Improving the Overall Balance between Supply and Demand of Labor
Strategic Thrust 6	**Spearheading Economic Redevelopment**
Program 11	Multi-agency Task-force on Economic Redevelopment
Strategic Thrust 7	**Maintaining International Competitiveness**
Program 12	Establishment of a Competitiveness Monitoring Group
Strategic Thrust 8	**Reducing Vulnerability**
Program 13	Establishment of a Scenario Analysis Group
Program 14	Strengthening the Home-based Character of Multinational Companies
Program 15	Encouraging a Positive Mindset in Government Agencies towards Local Enterprises
Program 16	Reviewing Institutional Support for Local Enterprises

Implementation of the Strategic Economic Plan

Program 17	Performance Indicators

Chapter 9

Social and Political Changes in Shanghai

Xie Xide

A few years ago transportation, housing and pollution were considered to be the major headaches for mayors of Shanghai. What are some of the major changes and challenges now?

From Renting Houses to Buying One's Own House

During the past five years many houses that were dark, and poorly ventilated have been demolished; and replaced by high-rise buildings, department stores, and elevated highways. It is hoped that by the turn of the century, the average space of residence per person will reach 10 square meters. Ninety percent of the residents can enjoy the use of gas for cooking; most of the new houses will be provided with running water, better ventilation and electricity. Many people have been assigned to houses in the newly developed area of Pudong (east of the Huangpu River) or in the suburb of Shanghai. However, the reallocation of housing was by no means easy, people still have the tendency of being reluctant to move. There is an old saying: "People would rather have cots in the west of Huangpu River than having houses in the east of the river." With the changes in the suburb and the newly developed areas, the reallocation has been carried out relatively successfully, though it will still take some time to overcome the difficulties of not having enough good schools, hospitals, shopping and recreational centers around the new residential districts. To raise funds for building the new housing, residents were encouraged to buy houses rather than paying low rents to the government as was done for many years previously. Through the money obtained from selling houses and a matching fund, the Municipal government was able to construct about 35.26 million square meters of new houses during the past five years, and about 1.4 million families have moved into new homes. At present, the area occupied per person in the urban area has reached eight square meters.

Eating Through a Common Rice Bowl or Participating in a Competitive Job Market

During the past five years, hundreds and thousands of workers from other provinces have come to Shanghai participating in the construction of elevated highways, bridges, the inner ring roads, and new buildings as well as working in various labor intensive jobs in factories and farms. The length of employment was determined by contracts signed and none of the workers are tenured as in the old days. Those migrants have played an important role in the construction and farming for the city although some have been blamed for some of the crimes and begging around the city, and for violating family planning rules and congesting rail transportation during the New Year holiday.

While many workers come from other provinces, some of the Shanghai workers were discharged from some state owned big and medium sized enterprises which were not profit-making in a competitive market. Those workers were given small amount of wages on which they could hardly survive. Some are encouraged to find new jobs or start various jobs in the tertiary sector. Re-education and reallocation of those workers for new jobs are challenges for the Municipal government; for example two years ago, some female workers were recruited to serve as air hostesses of Shanghai Airlines after screening a large number of applicants and necessary retraining.

Preparing for the Rainy Days Through the Insurance System

Chinese employees in the urban area have enjoyed socialized medical care since 1949. Together with the rapid increase of population, and the increasing cost of modern diagnostic and medical facilities, expenditure of social medical welfare has increased tremendously and become a big burden to the Municipal Government. Various proposals and programs have been worked out to modify the existing system for individuals, employers and the government to share the cost through group insurance. However, the proposals are still being reviewed and few modifications have been implemented. It is hoped that some reasonable details of the insurance system can be worked out this year.

With socialized medical care and reduced infant mortality, life expectancy for people has increased to about 76 years; the percentage of the aged has increased accordingly. For many state owned old and big enterprises, one of the major expenditures is on wages for the retired workers. In China, income for workers and employees consists of basic salaries which vary according to ranks, stipends of various sorts, and bonuses. For some workers and employees, their basic salary only accounts for a small portion of their income whereas for the retired, their only income is the basic salary which is not very high and cannot follow the inflation or the rise in the index of market prices. Therefore it is urgent to start some kind of social insurance system so that both the employees and employers can build up a fund for wages after retirement. However, the new system can only be implemented for new workers and employees. Some philanthropic foundations established in recent years have taken the responsibility of helping the aged and those who need special care.

Unequal Rates of Income Growth Allowing a Portion of the Population to Get Rich First (While at the Same Time) Not Widening Too Much the Gaps between the Rich and the Poor and the East and the West of the Country

It was encouraged since the early 80s to allow a portion of the population to get rich through honest means; and quite a number of people with good entrepreneurship did get rich through their talent and spirit of adventure. Since an efficient and sound tax system has not yet been established, quite a number of people became rich by not paying the right amount of income tax. If the gap between the rich and the poor becomes wider, it will not be good for the stability of the society and it has become an issue of much concern. With the fast economic development of the coastal region , the discrepancy between the eastern and western parts of the country is widening. There are 75 Kentucky Fried Chicken's and 63 McDonald's in 28 cities, while there are still about 65 million people living under poverty, the number of which is planned to be basically eliminated by the turn of the century. The issues for narrowing the gap between the rich and the poor and that between the East and the West are of major concern and crucial importance for maintaining the stability of the country.

Political Changes

In order to build up a good Socialist Democratic system which will be suitable to Chinese reality, there are still many things to be done such as the establishment of a sound legal system and the upgrading of the educational level of the entire population. Things should be done through proper legal processes rather than through relations with the authorities of respective bosses. Various laws and rules should be observed rather than being violated. With such a huge population, the observance of law can only be implemented by raising the education level and quality of the people, rather than just by imposing penalties. Decisions on major policies should be made after detailed consultations and discussions among the people concerned. A positive example of this process is evidenced in Shanghai where various proposals for housing reform have been extensively discussed before its final implementation.

In recent years the Standing Committee of the People's Congress at different levels have been busily involved in formulating various laws, with the local level focusing more on the details of the laws which are more suitable in their own situations. Moreover, the Chinese People's Political Consultative Conference (CPPCC), which consists of members from over 30 sectors and eight parties (in addition to the Communist Party members and a small number with no party affiliation), together with local branches have participated in offering suggestions and proposals to appropriate authorities on ways to resolve pressing political and social concerns. All proposals are usually seriously reviewed by respective authorities and many of them have been implemented. Many subjects are discussed during the annual meetings of both the People's Congress and the CPPCC. They include ways to combat corruption, improve personal safety and security, and reduce crimes, means to reinvigorate the state-owned large and medium sized enterprises, funding possibilities for the development of agriculture, education, science and technology, and challenges to bridge the gap between the rich and the poor as well as that between the East and West.

Reform and liberated policies have brought forward much needed progress to China in many areas. However, we are also witnessing the reappearance of pre-1949 social ills such as prostitution, racketeering, drug-taking, and the presence of contemporary problems, such as a few cases of AIDS. We have a long way to go and there are tremendous tasks to be tackled as we move to reach the goals of our ninth Five-Year Plan and to fulfill our long-term vision for the year 2010.

Chapter 10

The Recent Socio-Political Change in South Korea

Bae Ho Hahn

Korean Domestic Progress

Today, Korea is entering a new phase in its historical development. It has progressed sequentially from hermit kingdom to colonial dependency through an impoverished war-torn state, and now becoming a major independent force in international commerce. As the world's 12th largest economy, it is formally entering the ranks of the industrialized nations through membership in the OECD. As it has expanded economically, it has also achieved the long-awaited goal of democratization of its political system.

Throughout the post-independence period, the democratization process in Korea has been an arduous and at times a painful process. In fact, instituting a liberal Democratic Government in a country like South Korea has not been an easy task. What started out as a parliamentary democracy in 1948 began to erode during the Korean War and shortly thereafter changed into an authoritarian rule. The First Republic led by Syngman Rhee was toppled in April 1960 by a student uprising and in its place a parliamentary form of government headed by Chang Myon moved in. The Second Republic lasted only nine months when it was overthrown by a military coup led by General Park Chung Hee in May 1961. Thus Korea's experience in liberal democracy has been punctuated by a series of abrupt political changes that resulted only in more repressive rules.

Both the Park and the Chun military regimes applied, during their existence, severe and consistent coercion to broad segments of the population. The worst act of repression committed by the Chun regime was the massacre of civilian protestors who were fired on by paratroopers sent in by a military junta led by General Chun Doo Hwan in May 1980. The demand, from the families of victims of the massacre, to redress their grievances and to administer justice against those directly responsible for the massacre placed an unbearably heavy burden on the newly installed Kim regime.

This was the context within which the Kim Young Sam government assumed power and began to implement a series of reform measures. One of the toughest decisions he had to make was to return the military to the barracks from nearly four decades of involvement in politics and to eliminate a number of general-rank officers who were branded as "political" by their fellow officers. Another difficult decision he had to make was the problem of dealing with the repressive acts perpetrated by the ruling elite during the military authoritarian regime. Naturally, the Kim government could not ignore the Kwangju issue because the memories of the massacre were too horrible and fresh to sweep aside. Yet, for fear that a hasty decision against the perpetrators of the Kwangju incident might incur serious repercussion in Korean society and more specifically within the armed forces, Kim stated publicly that the Korean people should not forget what happened in Kwangju, but they should let history be the judge of the incident. For this he was critized by the opposition and those demanding a clean-cut settlement of the issue.

Later this year, however, a situation presented itself which President Kim could exploit to his own advantage. Shortly after the inauguration of the Kim government, it adopted a reform policy of abolishing the practice of depositing money under pseudo-names and made it mandatory that all depositors reveal their true identity if they deposited money under pseudo-names or when they open new bank accounts. In the process of implementing this reform policy, it was disclosed that Roh and Chun had concealed an enormous amount of cash under pseudo-names. By mustering political and personal courage to impose judgement upon the leaders of the two previous military regimes, Kim decided to prosecute two former Presidents, Chun Doo Hwan and Roh Tae Woo. The money deposited under pseudo-names was held against them as hard evidence of corruption although the two former presidents claimed that the money was donated by the business community for use as Ufunds for governing the country.

The two former Presidents were arrested on a charge of corruption, but, at the same time, another charge was imposed on them by the former Army Chief of Staff who was taken captive by the coup forces in May 1980 and who had filed, after the inauguration of the Kim government, a lawsuit against Chun and his coup planners on a charge for treason and plotting a civil war. A trial is now underway with due process of law guaranteeing the rights of the two defendents. So far, the defendents deny any act of treason or a plot for a civil war, and try to justify their actions for firing upon civilians in Kwangju and for taking over the government by force as an act that was inevitable in a chaotic situation created in the aftermath of the assasination of former President Park Chung Hee in October 1979.

The task which Kim Young Sam confronted when he assumed power in 1993 was to complete the process of transition toward democracy and to consolidate a democratic political order in Korean society. Consolidation of democracy would imply different things to different people. For us, suffice it to say that a state would be regarded as democratically consolidated if it succeeded in eliminating anti-democratic, extreme forces of the left and the right. This process is still in progress and the Kim government has been making efforts to establish itself as a regime which can claim full legitimacy as a duly elected, democratic regime.

Two elections held during the incumbency of President Kim Young Sam — a local governmcnt election in the summer of 1995 and a general election of the National Assembly (legislative body) in the spring of 1996 — helped to weed out the staunch protagonists of military rule, and provided the Kim government occasions to demonstrate its firm commitment to democracy and to broaden the bases of support for a democratic political order, thereby helping the Kim government to subdue the strength of anti-democratic extreme forces on the left and the right. There are still remnants of hard-line pro-authoritarian elements as well as Marxist leftist groups which expressly support the North Korean Communist regime. Their numbers are expected to dwindle over time as the democratic regime of President Kim Young Sam makes further progress with socio-political and economic reforms which will broaden the popular basis of support for the regime.

Despite his relentless efforts to carry out much needed reform measures in socio-political as well as in economic areas, President Kim is not without many obstacles and constraints which pose serious challenges to his rule and also to the future of Korea's democracy. The challenges that constrain Kim's efforts to consolidate a democracy in South Korea are not limited to the problem created by the presence in Korean society of extreme forces on the left and right. The more serious structural problem that constrains Kim's reform politics and the process of democratic consolidation is the absence of a well established party system.

A distinction must be made here between established and non-established party systems. A party system (in the plural sense) is considered "established" when it has reached a certain level of institutionalization and when organizations and not persons dominate the operation of the party. Presently, political parties in Korea are basically alliances of diverse groups and factions. They are dominated by the leaders of those parties who founded them. They undergo a constant flux when party leaders decide to sever their former affiliations and start new parties to satisfy their personal interests. Even the ruling party, which Kim Young Sam inherited from Roh Tae Woo although he later changed its name, is in essence an amalgamation of two large factions — one consisting of the former followers of Chun and Roh, and another consisting of the followers of Kim Young Sam. An intense intra-party conflict within the ruling party severely limits the Kim govemment's efforts to carry out a comprehensive political reform aimed to eradicate past ills accumulated during the extended military rule. Often the ruling party's interest comes into conflict with the government policies since rigorous implementation of a reform measure may lead to undermining the positions and power bases of the supporters of discredited authoritarian regimes.

Even though the major opposition party, the National Congress, is committed to democracy and its leader, Kim Dae Jung, was the major victim of the repressive rule of the past military regimes, the ruling and opposition parties have not succeeded in establishing rules and procedures, which are another hallmark of an established party system, for inter-party political competition. The opposition criticize the President for indulging in pratices that smack of the past authoritarian military leaders who often resorted to outright oppresive actions. Although both Kim Young Sam and Kim Dae Jung, the two life-long opposition leaders who fought against military rule, share their commitment to democracy, they have yet to accept rules and procedures of parliamentary politics where the major and minor parties engage in the politics of compromise and tolerance.

The State-Society Relations

Another way of looking at the current socio-political change in South Korea is to recognize the changing nature of the state-society relations. During the military authoritarian rule, the state in Korea came to dominate society so much so that one leftist-oriented Korean scholar characterized it as "over-developed". In fact, the state had a predominant place in the Korean political tradition, since the Confucian monarchical state as a patrimonial state virtually ruled Korea for more than 500 years, until Korea's annexation to the Japanese empire in 1910. There had long been a tradition for a strong, monopolistic state in Korea and this tradition was further strengthened during the Japanese colonial rule when a Japanese governor-general governed the colony with a well-organized bureacracy. Despite the efforts of the U.S. government to introduce a change to this tradition when it occupied Korea for three years immediately after the Second World War, it did not succeed in creating institutional bases for a pluralistic, conciliatory form of government as it intended.

During the Korean War, whatever democratic elements left in the U.S.-imposed governing structure of The First Republic headed by Syngman Rhee evaporated and the state reverted to its original, highly monopolistic and authoritarian nature. The massive drive for rapid economic growth undertaken by the Park regime in the early 1960s could succeed, in part, since there existed a highly centralized, well-established bureaucracy that set a series of policy guidelines and had exercised an exclusive control over the private business sector. The ruling elite during that period held a firm belief that rapid economic development required political stability and political stability could be had only when the state maintained tight control over the civil society. In other words, authoritarian rule alone would expedite the process of economic development and autonomies of civil organizations, intermediary groups, and other social institutions would jeopardize this process.

The export-led economic development strategy of the Park regime throughout the 60s and 70s resulted in the creation of a number of business conglomerates since the government placed heavy emphases on the development of heavy-chemical industries and large business firms that came to be known as "jaebul" were the major beneficiaries of this developmental strategy. The Park regime continued to hold a tight grip on those business conglomerates and could exercise effective control over them, but by the early 80s, during the Chun regime, the government began to lose its control over them as it pursued a policy of providing more autonomous powers to the private business sector. Today, state-business relations are drawing serious attention from both domestic and foreign sources and, with growing tension between them, there is a need for balance between business autonomy and governmental regulation.

The need for balance between state and society relations is not confined to relations between state and business. Democratization means the process whereby the rules and procedures of citizenship are either applied to political institutions previously governed by other principles (coercive control, social tradition, or administrative practice), or expanded to include persons not previously enjoying such rights and obligations, or extended to cover issues and institutions not previously subject to citizen participation. By trivializing citizenship and repressing political identities, authoritarian rule destroys self-organized and autonomous defined political spaces and substitutes for them a state-controlled public arena in which any discussion of issues must be made in codes and terms established by the rulers. In other words, democratization requires a change in the state-society relations in favor of the civil society. In this case, it is a resurrection of a civil society that was virtually on the verge of suffocation during the successive military rule.

Since the inauguration of the Kim government, there has been a proliferation of civic organizations and social groups which enjoy a far greater degree of autonomy than ever before. The labor unions are considered the most powerful interest groups that enjoy such autonomy. Under the authoritarian rule, the labor unions were severely repressed and the government made every attempt to maintain a tight control on the labor movement. It had only resulted in the upsurge of underground labor movements which seriously undermined the regime's stability. With the resuurrection of a civil society after the installment of a democratic regime under Kim Young Sam, the labor unions emerged as the most powerful interest group to the extent that a nationally controlled trade union organization can easily paralyze the Korean economy and disrupt the operation of such public utilities as subway systems and electric power companies. The democratic regime under Kim has fully legitimized the labor movement but it has yet to establish rules and procedures for institutionalizing modes for resolving labor management disputes.

The large number of civic organizations that sprang up since the liberalization of Korean society deal with a variety of issues that arose in Korean society as Korea underwent a rapid process of industrialization during the 70s, and as the consequence of the emergence of a new democratic order. Some civic organizations are preoccupied with problems created by the deterioration of environmental conditions while others are more directly involved in domestic political process such as election campaigns in the last two elections. In the last legislative elections a coalition of civic organizations acted out the role of a "watch-dog" for fair and clean elections by observing, and even investigating whether candidates conduct election campaigns properly according to the regulations provided for them by the Election Management Commission. Those who violated the rules were reported to the authorities and several candidates who were elected have been indicted and are now on trial.

There are a large number of civic organizations which are solely interested in such non-political issues as consumer protection program, educational reform program, and many programs related to the improvement of the moral standards of citizens. As the size of the middle-class Korean population increases, the current state-society relations shaped largely during authoritarian rule and backed by age-old Confucian tradition, is likely to undergo further changes that would reduce its lopsided nature and develop into a kind of relationship prevalent in pluralistic democratic societies.

The External Relations

The U.S.–ROK Security Alliance concluded in 1954 after the signing of the armistice of the Korean War has served as a fulcrum for maintaining peace and stability on the Korean peninsula as well as in the East Asian region. The Republic of Korea could achieve the so-called economic "miracle" because the security alliance could provide a shield behind which it could devote its energy to economic growth. Korea was not alone to benefit from the alliance. Japan was also a major beneficiary of this security arrangement.

Throughout the Cold War, Korea and the United States formed and maintained what many Koreans came to call a "special relationship". It refers to the strong ties and bonds forged through the experiences of the Korean War and further cemented by a long friendly bilateral relationship. Even in the uncertain and turbulent post-Cold War era, the U.S.–Korea security arrangement remains the cornerstone of the U.S. strategy toward the Asia-Pacific regime. Also Korea has been collaborating closely with the United States within certain regional economic organization such as APEC and more recently, in a summit meeting held at Cheju island, Presidents Clinton and Kim Young Sam made a joint statement to hold a four-party meeting consisting of the U.S., South Korea, North Korea, and China to discuss problems related to replacing the present armistice system with one that insures peace on the Korean peninsula.

Although U.S.–Korea relations have experienced some tensions and frictions over political and security issues, no other bilateral relationship has demonstrated such endurability and stability. The presence of some 30,000 U.S. troops in South Korea has been the major factor contributing to peace and stability in this region. The Korean government and the people of Korea regard them as the key element in the deterrent strategy against the highly mobilized, hostile North Korea. In fact, the combined forces of the U.S. troops and the South Korean armed forces are considered necessary to maintain a military balance between the two opposing and hostile forces deployed across the DMZ.

Next to the United States, Japan looms large in Korea's external relations. If the bilateral relations between the U.S. and Korea is considered more oriented to security and political issues, the Korea–Japan relations that came to be formalized after the signing of a treaty in 1965, is more exclusively economic oriented. After the normalization of relations between the erstwhile enemies in 1965, through the good offices of the Kennedy and Johnson administrations, Japan provided reparations to Korea as well as commercial loans. A large infusion of Japanese capital gave the Korean economy a strong impetus and led eventually to the achievement of a rapid economic development. Korea maintains a close economic relationship with Japan but the trade pattern has consistently been lopsided in favor of Japan and trade deficits toward Japan have never been reduced to this day. Maintaining a friendly relationship with Japan is viewed as essential for Korea's economic well-being. On security matters, however, Korea and Japan have not exactly shared a common view and interest. Korea does not regard Japan as an ally since the two nations are not parties to a security pact. While Korea is preoccupied with threat from its northern neighbor, North Korea, Japan is more concerned with regional security problems and trivialize the North Korean threat. Japan has sought to normalize relations with North Korea, but South Korea held tight to the position that Japan should recognize only South Korea as a legitimate state on the Korean peninsula This has often caused some friction and tension between the two countries.

After the collapse of the Soviet Union, Japan made a series of attempts to negotiate normalizing relations with North Korea until the North Korean nuclear facility in Yunbyun came to be disclosed and when the United States sought to impose a close inspection by IAEA on the North Korean nuclear program. Under pressure both from the U.S. and Korea, Japan recalled its negotiating team from Beijing where negotiations were carried out intermittently for a few years. Recently, after the signing of the Geneva Accord Framework between the U.S. and North Korea, Japan made another move to resume the negotiation with North Korea and of late North Korea has reportedly sent a middle-rank diplomat to Japan for consultation on this matter.

One significant change in Korea's external relations took place in the aftermath of the collapse of the former Soviet Union and its former satellite states. Secure under the protection of the U.S.–Korea security alliance, the Korean government under President Roh Tae Woo initiated what the press in Korea termed "northern policy", and established diplomatic relations with the former Soviet Union, PRC and several East European states. This was a major diplomatic breakthrough for South Korea where North Korea had exclusive diplomatic relations and which kept out South Korea throughout the post World War period. The recognition by Russia and PRC of South Korea as a sovereign state has greatly enhanced South Korea's international standing and worked positively for

South Korea to acquire a seat in the United Nations Security Council as a non-permanent member. The Korean peninsula is often regarded as a "powder-keg" in one of the potentially explosive areas in the world. The continued tensions and hostilities between two Koreas remain the major source of instability for this region but no possibility for improvement in the inter-Korean relations is in sight since North Korea refuses to sit at a negotiating table to discuss ways to reduce tensions and to promote means to achieve a peaceful resolution of the conflict. During former President Carter's visit to Pyongyang to meet the late President of North Korea, Kim Il-sung, it was agreed that Kim would accept Carter's proposal for holding a summit meeting between the heads of two Korean states. Carter's efforts to bring the two heads of states together did not bear fruit because of Kim Il-sung's sudden death in July 1994. In fact, inter-Korean relations further deteriorated after Kim's death and North Korea continued to refuse to resume talks at any level on the account that the South Korean government did not express condolence and forbade South Koreans from doing so in the South.

While the inter-Korean relations shows no signs of improvement, the North Korean food shoratage has become a matter of international concern. South Korea had sent them 150,000 tons of rice last year as a friendly gesture, hoping that it would open up the possibility for resuming contacts and talks with its northern counterpart. North Korea, however, reacted to this overture with a set of actions which infuriated the South Koreans. North Korea forced South Korean freighters carrying rice to hoist the North Korean flag in violation of an agreement reached in Beijing where it was agreed that South Korean freighters would carry the South Korean flag. Furthermore, North Korea arrested a sailor from South Korea who took some snapshots, accused him as a spy and detained him for a week.

The South Koreans were upset with what appeared to be an act of betrayal on the part of the North Korean regime. Under pressure, President Kim decided to withdraw his decision to continue to provide relief rice to the North Korean population. Instead of rice, which the South Korean government suspects that North Korea has diverted to feed the armed forces rather than civilians, the Korean government decided to send blankets and instant dry noodles through the International Red Cross which has been soliciting aid from the national bodies affiliated with it for humanitarian relief for North Korea. Through informal channels outside of Korea, North Korea has made frequent requests for rice from South Korea, but the Korean government maintains the position that it would not provide official donations of rice although it does not discourage private donation of grains from South Korea as long as it is certain that the rice is not diverted to military use.

It is the general consensus among observers of North Korea that, given the serious economic crisis North Korea is facing, no significant improvement or change in inter-Korean relations is likely to occur in the near future; although there are some indications that North Korea is making a painstaking attempt to meet the crisis by opening up its economy slowly to the outside world, particularly by inviting foreign direct investments in several special economic zones. The latest report shows it is now adding Pyongyang and two West coast cities, Haeju and Nampo to the list of such special economic zones. If this is the case, North Korea appears to be determined to follow PRC's strategy of modernization and economic development which would signify a sharp break from its earlier policy lines. The implications of this for inter-Korean relations would be far reaching and could possibly lead to some significant changes on the Korean peninsula.

PART III

U.S.–ASIA RELATIONS

Chapter 11

Challenges to U.S.–East Asian Relations

James A. Baker, III

It's a pleasure to join so many fellow Princetonians in such a beautiful city. As we gather here in Hong Kong, we can feel proud that our alma mater is holding this important conference on Asia in the Twenty-first Century. But, moreover, that it has chosen to do so here in the field.

Since leaving government in January 1993, I've been deeply involved in the creation of an institute for public policy at Rice University in my hometown of Houston, Texas. In particular, I am committed to making the Baker Institute a place where public officials, private sector leaders, and members of academia, working together, can bridge the gap between the worlds of ideas and action. It is a mission which possesses real urgency. And it is a mission which Princeton University has plainly accepted.

The inclusion of so many distinguished scholars and practitioners here today will allow us, I hope, to bridge the worlds of action and ideas — for they are worlds which have much to offer each other. The subject of this conference is no esoteric matter.

To talk about the next century as the "Pacific Century" has long been a staple of conventional wisdom both in America and here in Asia. The only question, it sometimes seems, is whether or not the "Pacific Century" has already begun. And a quick glance around Hong Kong would seem to render that a moot question.

Moreover, there is powerful evidence throughout East Asia that the *Pacific Century*, indeed, has already begun. Since 1965, the eight East Asian "stars" — Japan, Hong Kong, Indonesia, Malaysia, Singapore, South Korea, Taiwan, and Thailand — have averaged well over five percent real growth per annum. Their combined share of world exports of manufactured goods has risen from nine percent in 1965 to well over 20 percent today. Now mainland China — with double-digit growth rates in recent years — has joined this select club of "overachievers".

By almost any criteria, even with Japan's recent prolonged recession, East Asian economic performance has far outstripped that of the industrialized democracies of North America and Western Europe, as well as that of other developing countries. East Asia is, indeed, leading the world in economic growth.

I suspect that historians of the next century will identify this — the emergence of East Asia as a power center to rival North America and Western Europe — as one of the great historic phenomena of the last half of the 20th century.

I don't have to tell anyone here that the rise of East Asia has caused great interest and even some alarm in both Western Europe and the United States. Some see an inevitable cultural clash between the liberal "West" and the Shinto-Confucian "East". Other gloomy observers predict a division of the world into three great trading blocs vying for global mastery.

I am, frankly, unconvinced. I believe that the advantages of free trade far outweigh those of protectionism even if pursued on a regional basis. And I suspect that there is a stronger East-West convergence of opinion about core values (such as respect for the dignity of the individual) than extremists on either side of the human rights debate are prepared to admit.

Still, there are real challenges ahead as the countries of East Asia assert themselves in the international arena. And, though I don't want to denigrate the important role of the Asian *tigers*, I believe that relations between the United States on one hand and Russia, Japan and China on the other will be pivotal to the future of East Asia.

A discussion of American relations with the Big Three Asian powers is one that raises economic, political and strategic issues. Nevertheless, it's a subject that eludes conceptual clarity. Indeed, statesmen and scholars had enough troubles discussing the "strategic triangle" among the PRC, the USSR, and the U.S. during the Cold War. Trying to predict the future of what some undoubtedly will call the "New Power Quadrangle" is probably an impossible task.

So, mindful of the inherent complexity of the subject matter, let me begin our discussions with an overview of these three states and their relations with the United States. At the outset I should say (not as a politically partisan comment but as a statement of fact) that our relations with each of these other three powers are not as good or smooth as they were in the recent past.

Russia

Let me start with Russia — a country perpetually caught, it seems, in the dilemma of trying to determine whether it is European or Asian. It is in reality, I think, Eurasian — a true combination of European and Asian. Obviously, the United States has a big stake in the success of reform (both economic and political) in the states of the former Soviet Union, especially the Russian Federation. The same is true for every East Asian state.

Over the last year, we've seen several disturbing Russian political developments: Moscow's suppression of the rebellion in Chechnya, its point-blank refusal to cancel its sale of a nuclear reactor to Iran, its vehement objections to NATO expansion, and the resurgence of Communist and ultra-nationalist politicians.

These have rightly raised concerns in the United States and elsewhere. The possible emergence of an authoritarian, expansionist Russia is the stuff of nightmares for Russia's smaller neighbors — particularly its neighbors in Asia where Russian extremism has tended to take on a racist cast.

Nonetheless, it's important not to overreact to these events. A successful Chechen bid for independence would have wreaked havoc with the territorial integrity of Russia, a multinational state of 21 autonomous regions. It would have accelerated movements within Siberia for political autonomy (even secession) as opposed to "economic independence" which is already a reality.

Movement toward splintering Siberia from Russia would increase tensions with Moscow and, further down the line, tensions in the entire region! While some in the U.S. still cling to a contrary view, in my opinion, the disintegration of Russia is clearly not in the U.S. interest, nor for that matter, the interest of any state in the Asia-Pacific region.

With respect to Russian politics, we need to remind ourselves that Boris Yeltsin remains the first freely-elected leader in Russian history. While the results of the parliamentary elections in December would at first glance appear very foreboding, I think the real message is that democracy in Russia has grown strong roots. It is a measure of her progress that even Communist party candidates conceded the need to guarantee civil liberties.

Russian economic reform also presents a picture that is — on balance — positive. The deadliest threat both to economic reform and political stability — inflation — is down from over 1000 percent to roughly five percent per month. There has been enormous privatization — according to the U.S. State Department, better than 60 percent — and there is a new IMF agreement that commits Russia to an orthodox economic path. But, inevitably, campaign pressures will strain this commitment. And in some important sectors, such as the legal system, there has been little if any reform.

Nonetheless, there are now entrenched economic interests that will be very difficult for any future Russian government to ignore. A slowdown in reform, indeed, even some backsliding, is eminently possible, but there are forces and institutions in place that ensure Russia won't revert to central planning.

In short, a Russian future based on democratic government and free markets may not be a certainty, but it is much more than a pipe-dream. What we're most likely to see is continued muddling through, both politically and economically. This, of course, is likely to exacerbate the uneasy state of U.S.–Russian relations as Moscow grapples with the psychological problem of accepting its lowered status in the ranks of Great Powers.

China

Of course, Moscow's anxiety level is also likely to rise as a consequence of China's surge as the emerging Great Power — not just regionally but globally. I was in Beijing last October, and it is, of course, difficult to miss the economic boom that is propelling China forward. Indeed, that boom is creating some structural imbalances (particularly in trade) which will increase the difficulties in Sino-U.S. relations. Nonetheless, the key will be China's internal politics.

Beijing's transition in the post-Deng era will have vast ramifications not just for China itself but for the broader region. Deng's two-tracked approach of economic liberalization combined with political authoritarianism has yielded remarkable short-term economic results. It remains to be seen, however, whether it is sustainable in the long-run. The history, not just of the West, but of countries like Korea and Taiwan, clearly indicates that the creation of an entrepreneurial class inevitably leads to increased demands for broader political participation.

What will happen in the post-Deng era is a question that seems to be on the mind of much of the world. Some have suggested four possible scenarios. The first is that the transition has already occurred and that the current leadership will continue to preside over an economically booming and politically stable, but very authoritarian China well into the future.

The second, and I think most likely, scenario is a period of calm, lasting perhaps several years, as the leading figures of the new generation share power. Then internal jockeying will begin, and a transition to China's new generation of entrepreneurial leaders in their fifties will take place accompanied by some increased political freedom and reform.

A third (but I think unlikely) possibility is the emergence of a military dictatorship prepared to suppress political discontent even at the cost of foreign investment. Such a dictatorship could turn to foreign adventurism to rally support.

Perhaps even more dangerous is a fourth possibility: for power to devolve to the regions with a repeat of the unhappy experience China knew during the 1920's. Economic liberalization has already led to degrees of regional autonomy unheard of in recent Chinese history. And this trend could conceivably accelerate, in the absence of a strong central government, into outright conflict between competing centers of authority. China has managed to avoid the trends we have seen in the former Soviet Union and Eastern Europe toward regionalization and separatism and their attendant conflicts, and my view is that she will do so in the future as well.

As I mentioned, there is of course intense interest (not just in the Pacific but around the world) in what course China's development will take. This is so not least because China is one of the world's military powerhouses with three million men under arms and with nuclear weapons capabilities. In the unlikely event that China's development should include a bid for regional hegemony, only Japan in East Asia possesses the combination of population, technology, and economic might necessary to check such a bid. Yet, for powerful reasons — associated both with its constitution and East Asia's tragic history of the 1930's and 1940's — Japan today simply cannot play such a role.

This does not mean that Japan should forego a more assertive global role. Indeed, Japan should assume greater leadership internationally. But it does mean that the United States' military presence in the Far East will serve as an irreplaceable force for stability through the end of this decade and beyond.

Our special defense relationships with Japan and South Korea remain linchpins of Asian security. So, too, does our close military cooperation with the countries of ASEAN. Now, let me stress one point: I am not in any way suggesting or proposing an American-led alliance against China. Nothing could be more counterproductive. And I am not suggesting that our policy of engagement with China should become one of containment of China.

In fact, the growing economic links between China and the outside world — particularly the foreign investment that has driven much of China's recent expansion — represent by far the best guarantee that China will be a force for stability in the region. But maintaining a credible American military presence in the Pacific too, can play a role as it has in the past in promoting stability in East Asia and in discouraging or preventing conflicts that would not involve China. This is of course particularly true with respect to the continuing risk of conflict on the Korean peninsula where North Korea's game of nuclear cat-and-mouse with the international community appears to have paid off.

The United States and its allies in East Asia plainly have a powerful interest in China's long-term stability. And that stability, I believe, is best served by an approach that balances support for greater political freedom in China with continued efforts to deepen Beijing's economic links with the outside world.

Unfortunately, the Clinton Administration has had its difficulties in maintaining such a balance. After attacking the Bush Administration for "coddling dictators", the Clinton Administration came into office trumpeting human rights concerns to the exclusion of all others. Then, it waffled and reversed course on MFN (Most Favored Nations status). So it's not surprising that U.S. relations with China are strained. The only consistency in our policy has been a continuing inconsistency! Consider, for example, the process by which a visa was granted to President Lee Tenghui of Taiwan — first we assured China it wouldn't happen, then the PRC had to learn that it did happen from the Taiwanese press!

Our lack of consistency and discipline in our policies in Asia toward China, Japan, and North Korea has unduly increased nervousness in the region about American resolve, credibility, and engagement. More than anything, the states of East Asia, especially the thriving "stars" of ASEAN and APEC will be looking to Washington for reassurance that America will remain engaged in the Pacific.

So what should U.S. policy toward China be? Let me suggest a six-part policy approach that requires a careful balancing of our interests and values. First, the Administration should continue constructive engagement based on mutual respect and understanding.

Second, it should continue that engagement on the basis of the three communiques and the Taiwan Relations Act. It is important to reassert our policy that there is one China and that Taiwan is a part of China. But, also important is the reality that the U.S. will have broad unofficial relationships with Taiwan and will support any peaceful resolution of the differences between Taiwan and the PRC.

Third, the Administration should have a serious, on-going, high level political dialogue with China to reconcile differences over trade, proliferation, and human rights.

Fourth, the Administration should negotiate a bipartisan accord with our own Congress (as we in the Bush Administration did in 1989 regarding Central America policy) so that the U.S. can speak with one voice on China policy. Sino-American relations need to be divorced from the domestic political debate.

Fifth, we should encourage our friends in Beijing and Taipei to concentrate on substance, not symbols. For example, by focusing on cross straits investment instead of the problems of a UN seat. We should encourage direct contacts between China and Taiwan. The problem will resolve itself as a *de facto* matter ultimately. A *de jure* solution is not in the cards in the near term.

Sixth, the Administration should avoid the false choice that our policy has to be either all idealism (human rights) or all realism (MFN). It can and should be both.

And lastly, we need to get our act together and stop blind-siding China regarding visas to Taiwanese while continuing to reserve the right to grant them for private, unofficial visits.

Japan

Balance will also be crucial if we are to meet yet another vital political test in the years ahead: The emergence of Japan as a world power. Japan, of course, has long been an economic superpower. Despite its recent recession and banking crisis, Tokyo is still seen as a model of economic development by much of the world. In three decades, Japan rose from the rubble of World War II to an equal economic partner with the United States and Western Europe. And the U.S.–Japan security relationship has been the indispensable cornerstone of stability in the Pacific for the last 45 years.

Now, of course, Japan's economic success has led to political troubles. We've seen that constant trade surpluses are no substitute for strong internal growth. Chronic trade imbalances exact a real cost in terms of internal living standards, and prompt international tensions, such as those between the U.S. and Japan in recent years.

Let me address this issue separately. As many of you may know I am no "Japan-basher", but neither do I soft-pedal Japan's trading transgressions. Yes, some of Japan's markets are closed, typically by non-tariff barriers. Yes, we need to be tough on them. And yes, if necessary, we need to take unilateral action.

But there is a right way and a wrong way to do this. Quotas, goals or targets are not the answer. "Managed trade" is not the answer. High profile public confrontation is not the answer. It is counterproductive. Quiet, but tough and determined, diplomacy is the only correct approach.

The sad fact of the matter is that for Japan the mercantilist chickens have come home to roost! The yen will continue to appreciate over the long-term and Japan's economy will continue to suffer unless she changes her ways. The dollar is not weak versus other currencies. There is no dollar problem — there is a yen problem! Having said that, there is reason to believe the economic troubles of the last two years have caused Japan to begin shifting towards a more balanced economic approach, one that stresses rising living standards for the Japanese people and not just export performance by Japanese firms.

Part of the problem in U.S.–Japanese relations lies in the fact that Japan has yet to assume an international political role commensurate with its economic power. Since the mid-1980's, however, Japan has been slowly but steadily expanding its international role. Japanese troops have helped keep the peace in Mozambique and Cambodia.

History to the contrary notwithstanding, I believe that the United States and Japan's neighbors in the Far East should welcome, and, indeed, encourage this development. A greater Japanese role through the United Nations system including, eventually, some sort of status on the Security Council can help ensure that Japan's power is a force for stability in the region and around the world.

It will take a concerted effort on the part of Japan's political leaders if Tokyo is to assume its rightful place in the international community. Economically, of course, Japan simply cannot continue to run over $100 billion trade surpluses with the rest of the world year after year after year. Ultimately, Japan must find a way to empower her political leaders with the real power and authority necessary to overcome the entrenched bureaucracy — particularly in the Ministry of Finance and M.I.T.I.

After 50 years of preoccupation with internal development it will require strong leadership to turn Japanese society outward in a non-mercantilist manner.

I might add that additional liberalization of international trade and investment is needed throughout the region. While there are signs of a new maturity in the East Asian economies, opening domestic markets and encouraging domestic demand must remain priorities. No area of the world has benefited more from free trade and investment than East Asia, and no region has such an important stake in maintaining it.

The Asia Pacific Economic Cooperation forum can provide, I believe, a powerful vehicle for trade and investment liberalization. APEC can be the hub around which free trade can revolve. APEC's annual meetings offer an enduring framework for states of the Pacific Rim to build on the accomplishments of the Uruguay Round.

It is particularly vital that APEC's approach be inclusive, not exclusive, and in this regard there should be no East Asian caucus without Caucasians! We have once before drawn a line down the middle of the Pacific — with disastrous consequences. Once is enough.

America

That brings me to my final point — a brief discussion of the special role of the United States as the world's sole Pacific and Atlantic power. If we are, indeed, entering the "Pacific Century", I see the United States as very much part of it — economically, politically, and strategically.

But America's relations with the great powers of East Asia are undergoing a radical transformation. For much of this century, our role in East Asia has been driven by considerations of power politics. During the Cold War, our policies were shaped by the need to check Soviet and Chinese aggression. Strategic considerations remain, of course, important. And we pretend otherwise to our peril. Indeed, I have suggested just how vital it is to retain a credible American military presence in the Pacific — as much for reassurance as for deterrence. And having said that, I don't believe any Pacific nation (except perhaps North Korea) if asked would name the U.S. as its principal security threat.

But just as plainly, other issues — economic ones above all — have acquired a new saliency in America's relationship with all the states of East Asia. And that relationship, particularly with Japan and the member states of ASEAN, has shifted from one of the United States as patron and protector to one of the United States as partner and, yes, competitor.

Finally, I would argue that neither the United States nor, I suspect, the nations of East Asia are yet fully comfortable with their evolving relations. But I think that this is perfectly natural during a time of such great transition. Misunderstandings should be expected. Tension will be inevitable. But also inevitable, I am convinced will be a final recognition on both sides of the Pacific of just how inextricably linked the destinies of East Asia and the United States have truly become.

Chapter 12

Asia–U.S. Relations: Politics, Economics and Culture

Gill-Chin Lim

Introduction

People in Asia are now living in a special time in history. They create new events, and the new events affect their lives in a dramatic way. Observations on current and future affairs in Asia cannot rely on the old orthodox view about Asia and the world. Dramatic events that have been taking place in Asia over the last few decades and particularly after the Cold War need to be interpreted from a new angle.

In the past, the destiny of Asian nations was shaped largely by the global superpowers — the United States and the former Soviet Union. However, the collapse of USSR in 1991 and the ensuing disintegration of the Eastern European bloc have significantly altered the way the superpowers influence Asian affairs. Furthermore, during the last few decades, Asian countries have achieved remarkable economic growth which is described as the Asian Miracle. Nations in Asia also established regional institutions for economic cooperation to seek desirable directions for Asia's future with a shared vision. The rapid changes in political and economic lives have also been accompanied by cultural transformations. The old view that Asian destiny is dictated unilaterally by the superpowers is no longer valid. The relationship between Asia and the world has become multilateral and Asia's influence on world affairs has been increasing steadily.

The main purpose of this chapter is to look at Asia–U.S. relations from the political, economic and cultural perspectives. Especially, I am interested in bringing cultural perspectives to the discussion of Asia–U.S. issues. Before the end of the Cold War, discussions of Asia–U.S. relations were dominated by political approaches. We also observed that, during that time, the majority of regional organizations concerning Asia–U.S. relations were security oriented. In recent years, economic dimensions have become the main focus of discussions. And we witness a proliferation of regional economic organizations. Although, at present, we hear more about political and economic events in the public policy arena, they are heavily influenced by cultural forces. In addition, from a normative perspective, any search for new directions in Asia–U.S. relations should be based on a sound cultural understanding among the parties involved. Without such understanding, political and economic interactions cannot lead to a mutually satisfying outcome.

I begin this chapter with a brief note on defining Asia in which I present a geographical concept of Pan-Asia. Although my discussion in this chapter deals mostly with a region smaller than Pan-Asia due to the limitation in current systems of information, I present the concept as a more useful framework to study Asian affairs in the future. Then, I pose the following four substantive questions on Asia–U.S. relations.

- What affected Asia–U.S. relations in the past?
- What will affect Asia–U.S. relations in the future?
- What should Asia and U.S. do in the future?
- What should Asia and U.S. do to promote cultural understanding?

The first two questions are descriptive, and the last two normative in nature.

Defining Asia

A typical Asian map usually covers the region between Pakistan in the west, Japan in the east, Mongolia in the north, and Indonesia and Papua New Guinea in the south. Asia defined in this way encompasses 25 entities — Pakistan, India, Nepal, Bangladesh, Bhutan, Sri Lanka, China, Mongolia, Myanmar, Thailand, Laos, Cambodia, Vietnam, Malaysia, Singapore, Brunei, Indonesia, the Philippines, Papua New Guinea; Macau, Hong Kong, Taiwan, North Korea, South Korea, and Japan. However, this map excludes the five newly independent nations in Central Asia — Kazakhstan, Tajikistan, Turkmenistan, Uzbekistan, and Kyhgyzstan. Also, discussions of Asia frequently focus mainly on countries in the Far East and South-east Asia but exclude India, Bangladesh, and Pakistan. I find these definitions narrow and not necessarily useful in discussing Asian affairs in general or Asia–U.S. relations specifically.

There is a broad definition of Asia. People in Istanbul, Turkey claim that Istanbul is the meeting point of the East and the West. If we agree with this claim and consider Japan as the far eastern end of Asia, we get a definition of a much bigger Asia having a long stretch between Turkey and Japan. By adding Turkey, Iran, Afghanistan and the five Central Asian nations to the typical Asian map, we get 33 members in what we may call Pan-Asia. Pan-Asia is a much more useful definition in discussing Asian affairs and Asia–U.S. relations, because the countries in this region are interdependent politically and economically. There are also some cultural patterns in Pan-Asia distinguishable from the western cultural patterns.

Politically, there are a number of issues concerning the regional and national security in Pan-Asia. Conflicts between China and neighboring nations including India, Pakistan's attempt to develop nuclear weapons, a large reserve of nuclear warheads in Central Asia among others all need to be analyzed in a broad Pan-Asia context.

In terms of economics, we must realize that the development of sub-regions in Asia need to be physically integrated. The countries in Pan-Asia are diverse in their potential and comparative advantages and can gain from spatially integrated development of their human and natural resources. It would be desirable to develop a contiguous system of infrastructure which coordinates excavation and procurement of raw material, construction of manufacturing facilities, and transportation of human resources and commodities. For an efficient allocation of resources, it is recommended to build a spatially linked network among regional entities and nations weaving Black Sea Economic Cooperation, the Central Asia, ASEAN, APEC, etc. In this regard, it is encouraging that at the 1996 ASEM meeting , a Trans-Asian Railway connecting Korea, China, Southeast Asia, India, Iran and Turkey was proposed. Eventually, the idea proposes a railway system which adjoins Paris and the Siberia Railway.

Culturally, Pan Asia is highly diverse. Its religions consist of Christianity, Islam, Hindu, Buddhism and Shintoism. Almost all countries speak different languages, and within each country we find a variety of dialects. Nonetheless, some of the values of Pan-Asian cultures are similar to one another. Cultural patterns of Pan-Asia is non-linear which is contrasted to the western linear cultural pattern.

What Affected Asia–U.S. Relations in the Past?

There were several major factors which affected, directly or indirectly, Asia–U.S. relations during the Cold War (Spanier 1992, Chomsky 1994, World Bank 1994).

First, the most important factor was the bipolar competition between the U.S. and USSR Policy makers and scholars in both the Western and Asian nations were worried about Soviet threats around the world. For the U.S., the USSR was indeed serious competition for the world hegemony. For a long time since the beginning of the Cold War, the U.S. and its allies in Asia firmly believed in the Domino theory — if a nation within a region becomes communistic, a neighboring nation would soon fall victim to Communism.

The second important factor was that the U.S. has been the world's strongest economic power and far bigger than those ranked second and third. The U.S. had the largest share of international trade in Asia, and was also the largest donor nation to the underdeveloped countries. As a result, the U.S. was able to exercise significant influence on Asian affairs almost unilaterally and quite often on domestic policy decisions of Asian nations.

Third, the four superpowers — U.S., USSR, China, and Japan — exercised heavy influence in Asian political and economic affairs. This was particularly true until the mid 1970s when mainland China was under Mao Zedong's rule and the war in Indochina was going on.

Fourth, as Gunnar Mirdal (1968) described in his *Asian Drama: An Inquiry into the Poverty of Nations*, Asian nations suffered from poverty, underdevelopment, inequality, and institutional weaknesses. Policy makers and scholars were skeptical about the development of Asian nations and many turned to the theories of dependency.

The fifth factor was cultural dominance of the western — U.S. — world. National and local cultures were overshadowed by western culture. Western fashion, sports, movies and music were more popular than traditional cultural affairs in many parts of Asia.

Under these circumstances, U.S. policies in Asia were made unilateral and primarily concerned with maintaining military security. Examples of these policies were the U.S. support of post-war reconstruction of Japan, engagement in the Korea War through the UN decision, involvement in the Vietnam War, and the foreign aid through the U.S. Agency for International Development and other donor mechanisms.

What Will Affect U.S.–Asia Relations in the Future?

Significant changes have taken place in Asia since the 1970's. These changes will continue in the future and alter many features of Asia–U.S. relations.

First, there has been remarkable economic progress in Asia exemplified by the Gang of Four — Singapore, Taiwan, Hong Kong, and Korea. They are the first generation NIEs (Newly Industrialized Economies) — sometimes called ANIEs (Advanced Newly Industrialized Economies). They are soon to be joined by Malaysia and will be called the Gang of Five. The second generation of NIEs is likely to include Thailand and the Philippines. Tables 1 and 2 present the features of regional organizations. ASEAN with seven entities is a small economy in comparison to other economic blocs. In contrast, the 16-member East Asia accounts for 22.4 percent of the world GNP. Table 3 clearly shows that the Asian economy has been growing faster than any other regions in the world. ANIEs grew faster than any other countries until the 1980's. The growth of these economies have been closely related to export. Their records of economic growth and export growth are reported in Table 4. Regional composition of export by APEC member nations is given in Table 5. Although not in every country in Pan-Asia,

Table 1: Features of regional organizations (1991)

	Population (million)	GNP (billion $)	GNP per capita ($)	Export (billion $)	Import (billion $)
World	5,385 (100%)	21,671 (100%)		3,477 (100%)	3,543 (100%)
NAFTA	366 (6.8%)	6,600 (30.5%)	18,034	584 (16.9%)	649 (18.2%)
EC	328 (6.1%)	6,018 (27.8%)	18,348	1,383 (40.1%)	1,486 (41.6%)
APEC[1)]	1,976 (36.7)	11,711 (54.0%)	5,927	1,394 (40.4%)	1,410 (39.5%)
East Asia[2)]	1,675 (31.1%)	4,846 (22.4%)	2,893	794 (23.0%)	726 (20.3%)

1) APEC member nations in 1993 except Mexico and Papua New Guinea.
2) 16 countries including Korea, Taiwan, Hong Kong, Japan, ASEAN (Brunei, Indonesia, Malaysia, Philippines, Singapore, Thailand), three Indochina Countries and Myanmar. These countries are the potential members of EAEC to be formed in Malaysia.

Source: Recited from Ahn, Byung Jick, 1995, *Korean Economy: Issues and Prospects*, Knowledge Industry.

Table 2: Features of regional organizations (1994)

	Population (million)	Member nations (#)	Area (Km^2)	GNP in current price (billion $)	GNP per capita ($)
EU	371	15	3,235	371	19,367
NAFTA	368	3	33,938	368	15,456
ASEAN	414	7	3,382	414	1,239
ASEM	2,128	18	43,365	2,128	6,380
	2,146	25	16,673	2,146	6,140

Source: IMF, 1994, *International Financial Statistics and Direction of Trade Yearbook.*

Table 3: Comparison of the rate of economic growth of East Asia (Unit: %)

Year	1960's	1970's	1980's	1990	1991	1992
World	4.8	3.6	3.0	2.2	0.9	1.7
Advanced Nations	4.9	3.2	2.6	2.2	0.4	1.7
Developing Nations	5.0	5.4	4.8	4.1	4.4	5.8
Middle East	5.7	5.9	3.5	2.5	3.9	2.5
Africa	5.9	3.8	2.4	3.5	2.1	2.1
East Asia						
Japan	10.5	4.6	3.7	4.8	4.1	1.1
ANIEs	8.8	8.7	8.6	6.7	7.0	5.3
ASEAN	—	7.1	5.4	7.4	5.9	5.8
China	4.0	5.8	8.9	5.2	7.0	12.0

Source: IMF, *International Financial Statistics* (1993 Edition).
East Asia: Japan which is one of the leading nations of APEC, four countries of ANIEs (Korea, Taiwan, Hong Kong and Singapore) approaching advanced economy, five ASEAN countries except Singapore following in the footsteps of NIEs, China which is experiencing high growth through opening of its markets.

Table 4: Rate of economic growth and export growth of ANIEs: 4 nations (Unit: %)

	Korea	Taiwan	Hong Kong	Singapore
Economic Growth				
1990	9.6	5.0	3.2	8.3
1991	9.1	7.2	4.21	6.7
1992	5.0	6.0	5.0	6.0
1993	5.6	5.9	5.5	9.9
Export Growth				
1990	4.2	1.4	12.2	9.4
1991	10.5	13.3	19.7	7.0
1992	6.6	7.0	20.8	1.4
1993	7.3	4.3	13.0	15.7
Trade Balance				
1990	–2,179	10,796	–26	3,159
1991	–8,728	12,015	–131	5,711
1992	–4,529	8,184	–303	4,711
1993	385	5,840	–263	—

Source: Bank of Korea, Department of Research.
Unit: For Korea and Taiwan, GNP Growth Rate (million $).
For Hong Kong and Singapore, GDP Growth Rate (Hong Kong: 100 million HK$, Singapore: million Singapore $).

Table 5: Regional composition of export by APEC nations (1993)

Export/ Import	World	APEC	Korea	ASEAN	China	Advanced Nations within APEC	U.S.A.	Japan
World	100	37.6	7.3	1.7	2.7	26.1	14.9	6.3
APEC	100	66.0	15.0	3.6	5.2	42.6	22.5	10.1
ANIEs	100	74.6	12.5	1.6	9.0	43.2	27.5	11.6
Korea	100	75.3	10.3	—	4.5	57.6	31.7	20.9
ASEAN	100	75.3	21.9	4.0	4.6	46.8	18.9	25.1
China	100	76.6	47.4	3.3	2.8	26.5	10.6	14.1
Advanced Nations within APEC	100	61.6	12.5	4.2	4.3	43.3	22.3	7.8
U.S.A.	100	50.3	10.4	3.7	2.8	35.9	—	12.4
Japan	100	66.5	19.7	6.1	7.8	36.8	31.7	—

Source: Global Strategy Research Center, 1993, *Economic Cooperation of Asia Pacific in an era of Block Economy.*

a large number of people in South-east Asia and the Far East have come out of abject poverty in the process of rapid economic growth. And efforts to improve the quality of living in the region continue.

Second, after the death of Mao Zedong in 1976, the People's Republic of China began her open-door policy in 1978. Under the initiative of Deng Xiaoping, China has pursued political rapprochement with U.S., Japan, Korea, etc. and actively implemented economic reforms (Chow 1994). As we can see in Table 3, China is one of the fastest growing economies in the world.

Third, the collapse of the USSR on December 8, 1991 was followed by disintegration of the Warsaw Pact. Russia, under Boris Yeltsin, opened diplomatic relationships with Asian nations formerly considered hostile, such as South Korea, and increased international trade with neighboring nations. Unless there is a return to communist rule in Russia, the CIS (Commonwealth of Independent States) is no longer a major threat to Asian security. Few believe in the Domino theory.

Fourth, the conservative U.S. domestic politics led by Newt Gingrich and his fellow Republicans will affect Asia–U.S. relations. The new conservatism has been attempting to reduce U.S. support for international activities. For example, there has been an attempt in Washington, D.C. to abolish U.S.-AID and USIA. A substantial amount of budget for international activities has already been cut. U.S. has stopped being the biggest donor nation. Its image as a big brother and the world policeman is disappearing, while an alternative model of alliance has not yet emerged. Overall, the Clinton government's foreign policy regarding Asia is considered inconsistent, confused and weak. They have also been criticized for their lack of cultural understanding in international negotiations. As we discuss the impact of U.S. domestic politics on Asia–U.S. relations, it should be also noted that Asian–American population in the U.S. is one of the fastest growing. U.S. Census projections show that the number of Asian–Americans will grow at a rate of 36 percent between 1996 and 2005. The extent to which they are connected to Asia and they participate in U.S. politics will affect American policy decisions about Asia.

Fifth, we are now observing noticeable political changes in Pan-Asia. Many nations are much more stable politically compared to a decade or two ago. Popular demands for democratization and social justice have been on the rise. Political reform has been demanded in Turkey, India, China and Korea. Taiwan has been credited for its democratization. Thailand is gradually moving towards a more democratic governance. Korea put two former Presidents in jail on corruption charges. Political struggle to democratize Myanmar (Burma) is still going on. Peoples' quest for democratization seems to be contagious. A domino effect of democracy is spreading in Asia.

The sixth crucial factor which will affect Asia–U.S. relations is cultural change. In Asia a combination of traditional cultural values and a new modern mandate emerges now. The Asian work ethic currently observed in many Asian countries is not what has been inherited from the past as pure Asian. Rather, a new work ethic is created to accommodate contemporary needs within the framework of traditional values. Cultural fusion (Mahbubani 1995) is going on in Asia.

These factors provide new opportunities for Asian nations to improve their governance and well-being. However, some old problems will continue to beset Asia and the U.S. For instance, tensions between North and South Korea, China and Taiwan, China and other neighbors (India and Vietnam), and Pakistan and India will not lessen in the foreseeable future. The U.S. should also pay attention to the growing anti-American sentiments which emanated among younger generations in Asia during the 1960's and 70's.

What Should Asia and U.S. do in the Future?

In spite of the fact that Asian nations have been relatively successful in nation-building and economic development, they have a whole gamut of *critical human problems* to deal with (Brown *et al.* 1995, Neher and Marlay 1995, Pernia 1994, Tessitore and Woolfson 1994). Policy-makers in the region need to struggle with the following problems.

- Poverty
- Balancing economic growth and income distribution
- Basic needs in food and housing
- Peace in the region
- Democratization
- Observance of human rights
- Corruption and institutional governance
- Environmental protection and trans-national pollution
- International migration
- Education and human resource development

The list of *critical human problems* suggests that many Asian nations have a long way to go in order to attain the goals of a civil society — peace, justice, equality and affluence (Lim 1995a, 1996; Lim and Lee 1993). Sometimes, however, popular writings praising the Asian Miracle conceal the serious and chronic problems in the majority of Pan-Asian countries. The achievement made in such groups as the Gang of Four should not create an illusion that all parts of Pan-Asia is prosperous and comfortable.

To solve these problems, people and leaders in the public and private sectors in Asia and U.S. should work together to enhance the degree and quality of cooperation in political and economic affairs. Cooperative ventures of such mechanisms as APEC must be strengthened. Lessons learned from the Miracle should be applied to other countries through multilateral cooperative schemes. Underdeveloped countries such as those in Central Asia should actively seek cooperation with nations in Pan-Asia and U.S. to spur economic growth and political reform.

But equally important as political and economic cooperation is promoting cultural understanding. The lack of cultural understanding prevents people from making effective communication and mutually beneficial decisions. Therefore, I conclude this chapter with a normative proposal for cultural understanding. This proposal is not necessarily limited to Asia and U.S. relations. It is a general recommendation for all human kind.

What Should Asia and U.S. do to Promote Cultural Understanding?

The end of the Cold War might have reduced the intensity of conflicts between the two superpowers, U.S. and Russia. But conflicts among nations and within a nation seem to persist and even grow. There is a compelling need to nurture cultural understanding among peoples around the world. Normatively speaking, harmony in diversity is the best long-term solution to peace and prosperity in Asia, U.S., and the world.

At the practical level, I propose increasing cultural and educational exchanges between Asia and the U.S. Regional organizations such as ASEAN, APEC and ASEM should device a long-term plan for cultural and educational exchange. This plan should contain a concrete budget allocation for programs which can be implemented. Educational institutions such as universities in Asia and the U.S. can be working partners with the regional organizations. This approach will be useful for universities, because universities in both Asia and the U.S. are eager to globalize their students, faculty, and staff through active exchange programs (Lim 1995b). Within the context of cultural and educational programs, workshops and other training programs in cross-cultural communication and management can be conducted for public and private sector employees.

Conceptually, in promoting cultural understanding, we need to proceed with a two-stage approach. At the first stage, we clarify the differences. At the second stage, we seek commonality or synthesize different elements among different cultures.

To explain cultural differences, I present the dichotomy between the Eastern and Western ways of thinking. An example is the case of writing an address of a person. In China, Japan, and Korea, a person typically put his or her address in the following order.

Country/Province/City/Street/Number

In contrast, in the U.S. and Europe a typical address shown on an envelope is shown as follows.

Number/Street/City/Province/Country

Eastern thinking begins with the biggest entity and ends with the smallest, while Western thinking starts with the smallest and concludes with the biggest. In giving a name we also observe a similar pattern. In China, the head of the state is Deng (family name) Xiaoping (given name). In the U.S., the President is Bill (given name) Clinton (family name).

The differences in cultural patterns between some Asian languages and English are also well-recognized. Kaplan (1966) and Dunlap

(1990) have demonstrated fundamental differences in the mode of thinking among different cultures. Kaplan discovered a divergence in cultural thought patterns among people of different languages and in implications for inter-cultural education. He makes it clear that teaching English to foreign students differs from teaching American students, and that cultural differences in the nature of rhetoric provide the key to the difference in the teaching approach. Kaplan identifies five main patterns: (i) English — linear and logical, (ii) Semitic — regular zigzag and disconnected, (iii) Oriental — spiral, (iv) Romantic — continuous zigzag with underlying linear progression, and (v) Russian — disconnected zigzag with underlying linear progression (Figure 1).

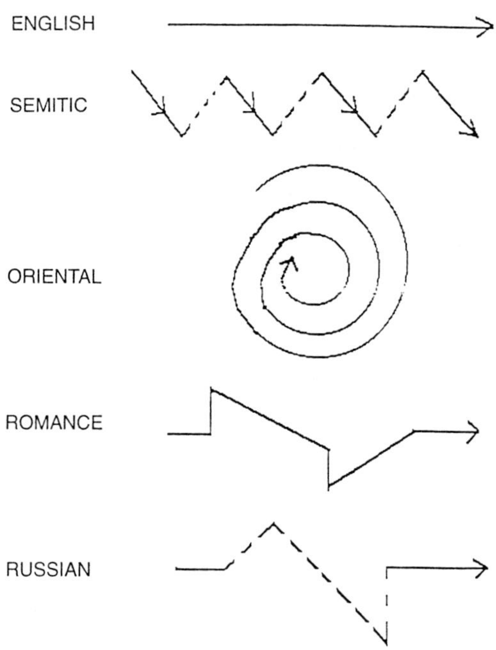

Figure 1. Cultural thought patterns in intercultural education.*

* Kaplan, Robert. Cultural Thought Patterns in Intercultural Education. *Language Learning* 16:1–20, 1966.

More recently, Dunlap studied the relationship between "Language and Power", in her experience in teaching writing to students from the Third World. Dunlap identifies five trends in Third World writing: (i) Conceptual Dissonance, (ii) Global Swingers and Encyclopedists, (iii) The Arabic Zigzag, the Hispanic Meander, and the Asian Spiral, (iv) Hidden Ideas and Self-Censorship, and (v) Grandiose or Bureaucratic Style. She also looks at the reasons for the lack of critical insights among Third World students in the U.S.

Furthermore, Logan (1989) showed that the differences between writing systems may have had a dramatic impact on the evolution of civilization. He suggested that the concrete, pictographic Chinese writing system developed a holistic, intuitive, and polytheistic civilization, while the linear, abstract, and non-pictographic Western alphabetic system has led to a scientific, rational, and monotheistic civilization. Logan believes both systems have problems. On one hand, Chinese technical competencies were not able to evolve into systematic development of abstract thinking and science. On the other, the western linear thinking has resulted in environmental predicaments and other ills of modern technologies.

These observations imply that cultural understanding could have a profound impact on international negotiations, problem solving processes and creative thinking. Investment in cultural understanding and global education — in schools, governments, business firms, civil assemblies — has more than an immediate practical value such as increasing international competitiveness. It can serve to cultivate people who can combine the best of the East and the West: *People who can think holistically, intuitively, rationally, and scientifically at the same time.* Such people will facilitate understanding across different cultures and be able to meet the challenge of *critical human problems* mentioned in our discussion more effectively and more humanely.

From a normative viewpoint, it is crucial to develop commonality among different cultures. Without shared common humanistic values among all people, we can never attain beneficial relationships among Asia, the U.S. and the rest of the world. When political and economic deals are made solely based on current costs and benefits and without essential cultural understanding, such deals will be short-lived. In such cases, the resolution of a conflict is only the beginning of another.

In general there are three cases of human interactions (Figure 2).

- *Separation*
- *Contacts without common values*
- *Commonality*

The first case is *separation*. People who are separated from one another do not understand one another, and do not have interaction.

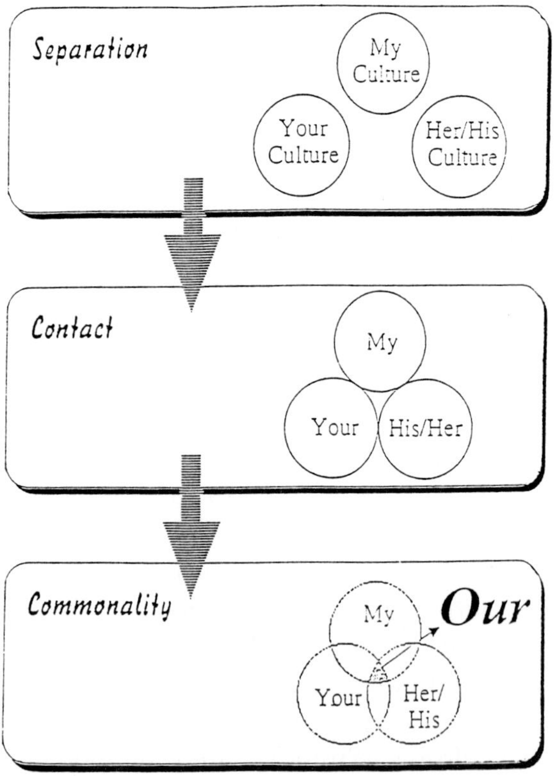

Figure 2. Three cases of human interactions.

People in the pre-Columbian world lived in separation. The early settlement policies for migrants in Hawaii was separation. In *separation*, there is no conflict.

The second case is *contacts without common values*. Different cultures do not understand one another, but they interact with one another. As a result, conflicts among people with different cultures arise. The conflicts among ethnic groups in American cities are good examples. The ethnic conflicts in India, the Middle East, former Yugoslavia, and Sri Lanka are a result of *contacts* without positive common values. The tension between Turkey and Greece is an example of contact without common understanding. The regional division within Korea is another case of contacts. U.S. negotiations with China, Japan, or North Korea are often a failure due to a lack of common values developed through cultural understanding.

The third case is *commonality*. People with different cultures share common values. The most important humanistic values to be shared include *peace, love, justice, equality*, and *affluence*. If people do not share humanistic values, we cannot develop an approach to solving critical human problems in a way which benefits all people around the world. When these values shape the common core of all people's lives, we can achieve regional as well as global well-being. The basic spirit of a civil society is founded on common human values. International organizations are also, at least nominally, designed to find sustainable solutions to critical human problems with the guidance of humanistic values.

Regional organizations, countries in Asia and the U.S. should invest in cross-cultural communication, negotiation and exchange programs for their people in both public and private sectors. Cultural understanding will make interactions in political and economic arena more efficient and humane. Particularly, we need more investment in advancing cultural understanding and sharing commonality among young people so that they can lead us to a brighter future.

References

Brown, Lester R., *et al.*, 1995, *State of the World*, New York, N.Y.: W.W. Norton & Company

Chomsky, Noam, 1994, *World Orders Old and New*, New York, N.Y.: Columbia University Press

Chow, Gregory, 1994, *Understanding China's Economy*, Singapore: World Scientific

Dunlap, Louis, 1990, Teaching Writing to Third-World Graduate Students, in Sanyal, Bishwapriya (ed.), *Breaking the Boundaries: A One-World Approach to Planning Education*, New York, N.Y.: Plenum Press

Kaplan, Robert, 1966, Cultural Thought Patterns in Intercultural Education, *Language Learning*, 16:1–20

Lim, Gill-Chin, 1995a, *Humanistic Planning for the Future: Synthesis of Planning Theories*, Seoul, Korea: Nanam Publishing House

Lim, Gill-Chin (ed.), 1995b, *Strategy for a Global University*, East Lansing, Michigan: Michigan State University

Lim, Gill-Chin, 1996, Homepage of the Program on Humanistic Globalization: http://www.ssc.msu.edu/~pohg

Lim, Gill-Chin and Man-Hyung Lee (eds.), *Dynamic Transformation of Societies*, Seoul, Korea: Nanam Publishing House, 1993

Logan, Robert, 1989, *The Alphabet Effect: The Effect of the Phonetic Alphabet on the Development of Western Civilization*, New York, N.Y.: William Morrow

Mahbubani, Kishore, 1995, The Pacific Way, *Foreign Affairs*, **74**, 1, 100–111

Myrdal, Gunnar, 1968, *Asian Drama: An Inquiry into the Poverty of Nations*, Middlesex, England: Penguin Books

Neher, C. D. and Marlay, Ross, 1995, *Democracy and Development in South-east Asia: The Wind of Change*, Boulder, CO.: Westview Press

Pernia, Ernesto (ed.), 1994, *Urban Poverty in Asia*, Oxford University Press for Asian Development Bank

Spanier, John, 1992, *American Foreign Policy Since World War II*, Washington, D.C.: Congressional Quarterly Inc.

Tessitore, John and Susan Woolfson (eds.), 1994, *A Global Agenda: Issues Before the 49th General Assembly of the United Nations*, University Press of America, New York

World Bank, 1994, *World Development Report 1994*, Washington, D.C.

Chapter 13

Vietnam in the Context of U.S.–East Asian Policy

Desaix Anderson

P. J. O'Rourke on page 333 of his book, *All the Trouble in the World*, writes of his excursion last year through Vietnam. O'Rourke interviewed a Vietnamese economist who described to O'Rourke his opposition to central planning. "The people who generate central planning's abstract theories are no longer important," the economist said. "You may think of sky and not know sky. You may think earth looks like sky."

The current transformation of Vietnam through "Doi Moi" is as fundamental as it is elusive in definition. As a one-time professor of Asian political economy, my greatest challenge since I arrived in Hanoi last August has been to understand the real nature of "market socialism". One senior Vietnamese official advised me that it was a market economy operated with socialist compassion, and it would be attained by 2020. Despite my occasional bewilderment over this development or that in Vietnam, I believe that his definition and judgment could be apt.

To carry out my assignment for today requires some analysis of the context both in Vietnam and of U.S. overall East Asian policy.

The Transformation: "Doi Moi"

Between 1986 and 1989, Hanoi was faced with self-described "crisis", with inflation running up to 700 percent and financial assistance from the Soviet Union evaporating. To meet the crisis, Hanoi adopted a series of major reforms redirecting Vietnam's economy to achieve "market socialism". Early on, households were given land tenure; private economic activity — restaurants, small shops, and household scale industry — was allowed to develop; Vietnam welcomed foreign direct investment (FDI).

Later, Hanoi also undertook structural reform and stabilization measures; orthodox International Monetary Fund (IMF) programs without the IMF: elimination of price controls and the state procurement system; liberalization of interest rates, currency devaluation and elimination of the dual pricing system.

As a result, inflation was cut in half by mid-1989 with a shift out of dollars back to the Vietnamese currency, the Dong. Hanoi cut budget spending (since it would have been difficult to raise an already weak tax base). This was achieved at least in part by reduction of military from 1.2 million to 600 thousand; reduction of workers in state enterprises by 800 thousand although there was very limited reform or privatization of state-owned enterprises; opening of trade and devaluation which gave farmers the added incentive to produce a bumper crop (25 percent increase in one year). Fortuitously, the start of oil production also helped.

Vietnam, like China, was an agricultural economy and manufacturing only constituted 13 percent of the economy. For this reason, renovation of manaufacturing industries in Vietnam was much more manageable than in eastern Europe.

Since 1989, more fundamental renovation has occured: 12 thousand state enterprises have been reduced through consolidation to 6 thousand; subsidies have been reduced substantially (to much less than China's). Manufacturing is growing at an average of 14 percent a year. Agricultural production grew more slowly, but still at four percent a year. Seven hundred thousand mom and pop stores sprung up. FDI (foreign direct investment) now totals $18 billion in commitments, perhaps $7 billion in disbursements, providing roughly half of invested capital investment for Vietnam. ODA from Japan is now about half billion a year; IMF/World

Bank another $400 million; ADB roughly $310 million. Overall growth has averaged 8.8 percent annually since 1988.

Vision of 2000 by the SRV — The 1996–2000 Five-Year Plan

Whetted by the success of "Doi Moi", Vietnam has grandiose ideas for its next five-year plan and even beyond as Hanoi approaches its 1000th anniversary in 2010 and Ho Chi Minh City its 300th anniversary in 2015. Hanoi's underlying goal is to integrate Vietnam into the regional and global economic system in preparation for the 21st century.

Hanoi plans to transform the landscape by the year 2000 by upgrading international airports, upgrading the northsouth route one and all major subsidiary roads, upgrading the northsouth rail link and upgrading seaports and inland water facilities. It is creating development triangles encompassing Hanoi, Haiphong, and Quang Ninh Province, and, in the south, Ho Chi Minh City, Bien Hoa, Ba Ria, and Vung Tau. It is strenghthening the universal health and education systems. It is trying to bring down the birthrate to 1.7 per female, while doubling the per capita GDP.

Fundamental Question is Real Definition of "Market Socialism"

Vietnam's ambitious plans for growth into the next century depend on attaining high levels of domestic capital mobilization and foreign investment. A fundamental challenge facing the Vietnamese government today — and a key concern for foreign investors — is how to create a climate conducive to aggressive foreign investment and robust domestic capital formation in the context of "market socialism".

The debate on this issue appears not so much over the direction of economic policy, but rather the pace and limits of ongoing reform. The government's commitment to Doi Moi is well-established. However, the means of achieving "market socialism", and to some extent its very meaning, are still being defined.

The work surrounding the highly important Eighth Party Congress scheduled for June 1996 on issues scheduled for June such as the role of state-owned enterprises, impediments to investment, and barriers to trade, will have profound implications not only for foreign companies operating and selling in Vietnam, but for the success of Doi Moi itself.

Will Vietnam follow the advice of the donors in Paris? The advice includes:

1) Greater effort to strengthen domestic resource mobilization;
2) To accelerate state-owned enterprise reform and to improve the environment for private sector development (now accounts for only four percent of manufacturing, but produces almost all new jobs);
3) Strong focus on rural development and human resource development — to ensure high quality as well as a rapid pace of growth, and to overcome urban-rural imbalances; and
4) Improvement in implementation of projects financed by ODA.

To this list, might be added needed reforms pointed out by Prime Minister Vo Van Kiet in addresses to the National Assembly in October 1995 and again this spring:

5) Further strengthening of the legal system;
6) Diminution of bureaucratic barriers to trade and investment;
7) Elimination of corrupt practices; and
8) Development of transparency in the functioning of the economy.

The jury, frankly, is still out. Vietnam is either poised to become the next Asian tiger, or to become just another also-ran and stagnate. A decision at the Eighth Party Congress to accelerate reform and the clear political commitment to implement continued reform would spur foreign investment and encourage Vietnam's nascent private sector. A decision to retrench or slow reform would raise major questions and even alarm in the foreign business community and Vietnamese-owned private sector, and would clearly affect FDI and domestic capital development.

The second great debate in preparation for the Party Congress is growing concern about the flourishing "cultural pollution" as Vietnam opens its economy and doors to foreigners. The more conservative view of "social evils" holds that pornography, prostitution, gambling, drugs, karoake bars (none of which, incidentally, was invented in the United States) were imported from the West. Overnight, in early February, in a hastily designed implementation of a law long on the books of Hanoi's Coca Cola, Kodak, Samsung, Sony, San Miguel signs were painted over, raising questions about Vietnam's attitude toward the foreign business presence and investment. Recently, a drumbeat of calls to combat "peaceful evolution", a "cunning plot to overthrow Vietnam's system", has reappeared in the military press. On the other hand, the chairman of HCM City People's Committee January 27, was quoted as saying forthrightly, "Pollution, unemployment, traffic jams, and social evils, are the result of increasing urbanization, and not problems for HCM City or Vietnam alone, but also for most of the world's major cities."

Vietnam, of course, has the sovereign right to protect its people from social evils, such as rampant commercialization and pornography and to preserve Vietnam's rich cultural heritage. The 20th century has plenty of examples of the costs as well as the benefits of rapid economic modernization. These anti-foreign undertones taken by some in these campaigns may be merely rhetorical hyperbole, but they also could be the efforts to change what is commonly thought to be the substance of "Doi Moi". This issue and continued progress on economic reform are obviously related and their impact on each other intertwined. The drama of change and the investment climate for foreigners clearly could be fundamentally altered by how they are resolved at the Party Congress.

United States–Vietnam

I have said little about the United States thus far, on purpose, because Vietnam has survived, reformed, developed, and undertaken the profound changes of "Doi Moi" without the United States' playing an active role — except through the embargo.

The United States comes to the scene after many years of alienation from mainstream Vietnam. As Secretary Christopher said last August 6, in opening the embassy, "With the Cold War over, we view Vietnam as a product of its own history and the master of its own destiny." That observation by Secretary Christopher was coupled with the notion that we should come to know Vietnam "As a country, not as a war." That signaled that the U.S. was now prepared to look to the future, to build a new relationship with Vietnam.

The United States normalized political relations with Vietnam in the context of America's overall policy toward East Asia and the Pacific. We seek a stable East Asia and Pacific at peace with its own peoples and at peace with its neighbors, devoted to building civil societies and seeking prosperity for its citizens.

Our historic commitment to such principles as democracy and universal human rights means that we will speak out on these subjects, but it does not mean that we intend or will try to impose our values on other cultures.

We now see Vietnam as very much part of contemporary Asia, rather than in isolation.

We wish to build relations with Vietnam, not as a foil against any other nation, but because Vietnam, a nation of 73 million people, is an important country in its own right, and will increasingly become an influential player in the region and around the world.

We also wish to build on the rich cultural and familial links between our two nations.

We have come to Vietnam to support its commitment to renew and reform in its own way and consistent with its own history and culture, as Secretary Christopher stated. Within the framework essentially of Vietnam's own reform "Doi Moi", we wish to construct a mutually beneficial relationship between the United States and Vietnam.

In the broader context, good relations between Vietnam and China, and between Vietnam and its South-east Asian neighbors, are in the interest of peace and stability in Asia and are, therefore, in America's interests.

U.S. Policy

As President Clinton has stressed, our top priority in Vietnam remains the fullest possible accounting of those personnel still missing in action from the Vietnam war era. The Vietnamese government understands this priority, and agrees that we must intensify efforts to resolve these questions. Cooperation has been excellent, reconfirmed at the highest levels during a March 11–13 presidential delegation visit to Hanoi.

At the same time, the United States wishes to move steadily to develop our relations with Vietnam across the board. We would like to foster agreements and regular exchange on trade, investment, agriculture, science, technology, culture, education, on strategic issues — in virtually every area of mutual interest and concern. Moreover, there are significant complementarities between our two nations and economies. We would like relations between the United States and Vietnam to be as normal as our relations are with Vietnam's ASEAN partners. This is our long-range goal.

We have begun intensive discussions with the Vietnamese government about normalizing economic relations between our two countries. These discussions resumed in Hanoi this week.

Our overarching goal during the coming months is to move toward a comprehensive trade agreement that would open Vietnam's markets to U.S. business and investors and ensure intellectual property rights protection, nondiscrimination, and remove barriers to investment in services, trade, and distribution. Such an agreement would also give Vietnam MFN status. On separate tracks, we wish to work toward agreements that would allow overseas private investment corporation, or OPIC, the Export-Import bank, and the trade development agency to begin operating in Vietnam.

We held talks in January to try to regularize Vietnam's official debt to the U.S. The Vietnamese government has reached agreements on debt rescheduling terms with all creditor nations under the Paris club, and is committed to reaching agreement with the U.S. as well.

Each of these agreements can proceed on its own track. OPIC and EXIM, for example, need not await conclusion of a trade agreement to be implemented, and vice versa.

Growing Economic, Commercial, and Other Ties

Even as we work to construct the formal framework for U.S.–SRV economic relations, our economic, commercial, and other ties are already growing.

We have made notable progress in our agricultural relations. The U.S. Agriculture Department and Vietnam's Ministry of Agriculture and Rural Development have set up a joint working group on agricultural cooperation in such areas as information and technical exchange, training, and policy review, with the intention of strengthening Vietnam's agricultural sector and increasing opportunities for exporters of U.S. agricultural products.

We are similarly prepared to move ahead with exchanges and training between our commerce and transportation departments and their counterparts. We are working toward a civil aviation agreement. Commerce recently led our first USG-sponsored trade mission to Vietnam and penned agreement on commercial law exchanges.

We are also cooperating in dealing with narcotics problems, and in customs training.

We have expanded our dialogue with Vietnam on regional, multilateral, and security issues, notably during East Asia & Pacific Assistant Secretary Winston Lord's January 18–20 visit to Hanoi. Our defense attache has been cordially received since arrival in December and we will welcome Vietnam' s attache in Washington later this year.

Although our official aid assistance is very small, the USG and private organizations — including NGO's, corporations, universities, foundations — are providing substantial assistance, scholarships, training, exchanges, and small scale health and educational projects. We strongly encourage such efforts.

Prospects

Of course, the success of plans for normalizing economic relations and expanding our trade and contacts with Vietnam depends in no small part on the continued progress of the Vietnamese in reforming and liberalizing their economy. Vietnamese officials uniformly tell us that this is their priority.

We also warmly welcome Vietnam's membership in ASEAN, one of the most significant developments in years in Asia. Vietnam's high interest in APEC and WTO signals commitment to multilateralism and bodes well for our bilateral economic relationship.

Moreover, U.S. proposals will be fully consistent with requirements for AFTA, WTO, and APEC, and agreement with the U.S. on trade issues will accelerate Vietnam's entry into regional and global economic organizations.

There are now over 400 enthusiastic U.S. firms operating in Vietnam. U.S. companies — individual entrepreneurs and multinationals, high and low tech — are taking a hard look at sectors across the board for trade and investment.

The U.S. moved from the number 14 investor to number six overall and the third largest in 1995. That's not good enough. We expect to become number one.

American companies are uniquely placed to prosper in the Vietnamese market. Many Vietnamese think that American technology is the best in the world, and they want to get more of it quickly. Not only do U.S. firms have the best technology, they also have superior management and marketing techniques.

Trade, although small, is expanding rapidly. U.S. exports to Vietnam in 1995 increased 47 percent over 1994 to $253 million;

Vietnam exports to the U.S. increased 400 percent in 1995 over 1994 reaching $199 million. Grounds for continued, rapid expansion of two way trade is evident.

There is no more fitting time for cooperation and communication between Vietnam and America. After 20 years of isolation from each other, economic cooperation can help overcome the distrust, misunderstandings, and myths which for so long thwarted the hopes of many Americans and Vietnamese.

But U.S.–Vietnam policy is not based on righting past wrongs or on romantic memories. It is based on a realistic appraisal of our national interests. Our focus and that of the Vietnamese is firmly fixed on the future of our relationship, not the past.

We will achieve the president's highest priority — fullest possible accounting for our missing in action from the War.

Good, solid relations with this emerging power of Vietnam will help consolidate our strategic partnership with ASEAN — a key grouping of moderate, dynamic, fast-growing and influential nations.

An important gap in an arc of our friendly, productive relations reaching from Japan, Korea, and Mongolia in the north through ASEAN to Australia and New Zealand in the far south will be filled.

Vietnam's integration into ASEAN and the broader Pacific community will end the historic anomaly which threatened peace and stability in the past.

Assuming that Hanoi remains committed to economic reform, Vietnam in all likelihood will enter the ranks of the tigers and dragons and represent a major and profitable trade and investment partner for U.S. companies, adding jobs in America.

The tortured intimacy of our past engagement and over a million Americans of Vietnamese descent can facilitate building of productive exchanges between the rich cultures, societies, and intellects of Vietnam and America.

The Vietnamese can speak for their own interests, but again, perhaps the insights of O'Rourke are pertinent. P. J. asked the Vietnamese economist if he were not worried about capitalistic exploitation of the masses. The economist first quoted China's

Deng Hsiao-ping's famous remark, "People were afraid if the window were opened, flies and mosquitoes would fly in." "But", the economist added, "with money we can buy mosquito repellent or screens."

Thank you once again.

Chapter 14

U.S. Policy Toward China and Indonesia

Stapleton Roy

Let me begin my remarks by pointing out that I am here in my personal capacity and not my official capacity. It is important to point this out because if our founding fathers had had the wisdom to found the College of New Jersey in 1741 we would have had a Princetonian as a Secretary of State when we have this conference. I have been privileged to serve under three Secretaries of State, in my diplomatic career, who have been Princetonians. Under those circumstances probably I would have been brought here in an official American aircraft painted orange and black for the occasion. I had a hair-raising experience getting here. I realized it was going to be hopeless to get Washington clearance for any official remarks to a Princetonian audience. My remarks reflect my own views only. I am very grateful to Secretary Baker; he, of course, was Secretary of State when I was sent as Ambassador to China and as I listened to his very wise remarks about China today, I began to reflect that there were so many similarities between his views and my views that maybe a Princeton education creates a certain similarity of thought patterns that makes conferences like this unnecessary — since we all think alike. It also occurred to me that if I ever became Secretary of State he would probably be very high on my list to be nominated for Ambassador to China. Now some of you may think Jim Baker is suitable for higher things. I would just like to remind you that based on recent experience there is a better than 10 percent chance that an Ambassador to the People's Republic of China will become President of the United States. So that actually, I had his own best interests in mind in doing so. Unfortunately, no Ambassador to China has ever become Secretary of State, so maybe my opportunities to nominate him to China will not be realized.

Our topic is the United States and Asia. Now, the Chinese have a saying that you should know yourself and know your enemy and you will win a hundred victories in a hundred battles. If we are going to talk about Asia I think we need to talk a bit about the questions of how the United States thinks about and responds to Asia. This comes naturally to me because I have served in recent years to two of the most populous countries in Asia. It has required me to do a lot of thinking about the question of how the United States is reacting to what is going on in Asia. I would argue that there is going to be a very difficult process in the United States of adjusting to the sorts of policies we are going to need to deal with the current world situation facing us. Because in many ways it is unique. It is not a situation that we have coped with successfully in the past. And we need to think seriously if we are going to be able to cope successfully with the problems that Asia is going to present to us in the future. Now why do I say that? The reason is because East Asia, as you have been hearing endlessly in this conference, is a unique mixture in the world. It has an advanced world-class economy such as Japan. It has a whole host of small and incredibly successful economies that in the space of two generations have essentially turned their societies from backward societies to near developed statehoods. But it also includes two of the three largest developing countries in the world — China and Indonesia, which together have a population of a billion and half people; a population that is double the size of that of the rest of Asia and the United States combined. Hence the question is whether the United States, in terms of our traditions and our ways of thinking, is capable of responding the way we need to respond to the problems of these large developing societies. That is going to determine, in large measure, whether we are going to come up with successful policies. I am going to develop this a little bit as I go along in my remarks.

On the surface we all know that East Asia is incredibly successful. Japan is a world-class economy; it has a capability to be a world-class military power. China has been developing in double-digit figures. ASEAN is one of the genuine success stories of the world. It has been a help in developing the rest of the world for decades now. And you can see the differences when you go down there. If current trends continue, obviously the next century will be the Pacific century. But, as all of you probably learned in your Princeton history courses, current trends never continue indefinitely; there are key question marks over the processes that are taking place in East Asia that could cause us to doubt that current trends will continue indefinitely. And, therefore, the real challenge for the United States is: are our policies going to be helpful in sustaining the current policies and trends in Asia as long as possible? Or, are we going to find ourselves reacting to certain aspects of those trends in ways that absolutely help to abort the process, and this is not impossible, and it is something we have to reflect upon. I just want to put some of these ideas out before you, because I think the purpose of a Conference like this is to try to get us thinking about issues that matter to us.

There are several factors about Asia that we need to think about. First of all, China has gone through an incredible economic revolution in the last 17 years. There have been very significant political changes in China in terms of the relationship between the government and the people of China. But it has not yet been reflected in institutional changes. And there are more worries about the future of China because of the institutional weaknesses and the rapid pace of economic and social changes there. These are healthy for a country that has the capabilities to become the strongest economy of the world, if current trends continue. But the institutional weaknesses remain. The same thing could be said about Indonesia. Here is a country that has had rapid economic growth and political stability for 30 years. It has also pursued policies of moderation and cooperation with its neighbors that essentially make the ASEAN miracle possible. ASEAN came into being because of the changes in Indonesia that represented the switch from confrontation to cooperation. ASEAN was founded in 1967 and it has been the changes in Indonesian policy that have enabled all of the positive trends to take place. Without that, you wouldn't have the current positive trends in South-east Asia. But Indonesia also has leadership transition problems and political institution problems which raise questions in the minds of Indonesians and foreign observers about whether the country is going to be able to surmount these leadership transitions successfully.

Another facet of East Asia, which is very important and we cannot forget. It has spawned three of the four divided countries that have emerged since world War II; two of those still exist and are the potential sources of tension here. As we have seen recently in the Taiwan Straits crises, situations that seem to be successfully stabilized can suddenly flare up again very rapidly. So we need to be very careful about making facile assumptions about current trends in East Asia. They can be reversed and they can be reversed very quickly, if the leaders in this region and if the leaders in the United States do not manage the challenges they are facing successfully. That is not something we can brush aside as impossible.

Another factor is that Asia is facing total uncertainty. Predicting the future of this region cannot draw on the lessons of the past. Now I invite you to our comparison of East Asia and Europe in this instance. I would argue (and this is a debatable topic) that if you look at what is happening in Europe, you can find that there are lots of parallels in past European history that are helpful in understanding what is going on in Europe now. There are some new elements such as the United States in Europe and the existence of the European Union. You see a Russia weakened by its own internal difficulties. You see a unified Germany now as a bulwark of the status quo in Central Europe which has emerged from the European post Cold War world. And we have the Balkans re-Balkanized. All of these are traditional patterns in Europe, and you can learn lessons from 19th century history and earlier periods.

East Asia entered the world of independent nation states barely 50 years ago. Virtually all of the southern half of Asia was under colonial domination for the previous hundreds of years until the post-World War II period. Then we were divided by the Cold War so that you did not have any unified Asian institutions. It was only three years ago in Seattle that the leaders of Asia were able to sit down together and talk — something we had been doing in Europe for decades, hundreds of years. In Asia it had never happened before. When the Emperor of Japan visited China successfully in 1992, that was the first time that an Emperor of Japan had visited China. So we cannot fall back on traditional Asian ways of doing things in terms of anticipating what problems Asia is trying to cope with right now. Now it is doing pretty well. ASEAN has shown that countries with disparate historical backgrounds, colonial backgrounds, cultures and ethnic backgrounds, have been incredibly successful in establishing patterns of cooperation in a short period of time that have made ASEAN one of the bulwarks of stability in this part of the world. So we don't have to be pessimistic in saying that we have to deal with the situation. But we do have to recognize that in Asia we just can't look at the lessons of the past, we have to keep our minds open.

The real question that we as Americans should be thinking about is, are our diplomatic traditions up to this challenge? I would argue that we need to do more thinking about that question than we have been doing so far. The reason for this is very simple, ostensibly, if you look at American history as we all studied it at our diplomatic history courses at Princeton. This century you can divide our involvement in the world into two phases, the isolationist pattern that has marked most of our history, nearly three quarters of it, and the interventionist period that has marked the brief World War I and the World War II and post- World War II period. But in both of those instances our intervention in the world was in a bi-polar situation. A crusade, shall we say, for freedom or right against wrong and that ended with the post-Cold War world. Now, another famous Princetonian has talked about the legalistic, moralistic traditions of American foreign policy. And those are alive and well today. Those traditions have worked fine when we were isolationist and they have worked fine in bi-polar situations which we saw as crusades between freedom and tyranny. But in the current world situation we are dealing with a number of power centers of different characteristics. Those various power centers around the world not only include highly developed countries like Japan or western Europe, but also Russia, China and Indonesia as potential future powers, who don't have traditions similar to ours, who are going through development processes that are going to be very troublesome at the key stages. And, if we try to play the balancing role in the world, try to use our powers to prevent new hostile groupings from emerging against us, falling back on our legalistic, moralistic approaches to dealing with these countries is not going to be up to the task. We need to think about whether there is a way without going to a type of *realpolitic* which is simply impossible in the American tradition. We need to find a better form of enlightened pragmatism for dealing with these sorts of issues, the types of approaches that Secretary Baker was talking about, and enjoy the support that they need to enjoy in the United States. But if you look at the current political debate in the United States you worry about that. Because that is not the type of world view that is being generated by our own political processes. We face the challenge, as a nation, of coming up with the domestic support for the polices that we need to be pursuing in East Asia; where we have to deal with the Chinas along with the Japans and along with the Taiwans and the Malaysias and Koreas and Singapores who are moving so rapidly in directions that are compatible with our interests that we have been able to deal with.

Now there is another problem here. When you look at East Asia you see that, in fact, economic development process out here in the smaller entities has produced political changes that cause you to be confident that if you can sustain economic development long enough, you can create the middle classes that become the underpinnings for the political changes, and the respect for human rights, that make their societies more compatible with their own governments. That's fine. But, let us remember that during the period when these societies were going through struggles and changes we were in the Cold War period, which fortunately lasted long enough so that they were able to go through the period of decades necessary to complete the process. The process still is uncompleted, but in Korea and in Taiwan and arguably in Thailand we have already seen the impact of rapid upheaval and development, sustained over time, on the political systems of these countries. And that's something we ought to be very encouraged by. But how do you relate this to the process of the China or an Indonesia? You can produce middle classes in China on the level of a Taiwan or a Korea or even a Japan, 250 million people in China; you still have 900 million people who aren't at that level. No political system in the world has had to struggle with the problem of how to take a giant mass of population, such as you have in these great big populations, and produce the political changes that come with the types of economic developmental changes that we want to see happen. And we need to worry about this. Because, we need a process that can sustain the positive changes long enough without being thrown off course by the problems that they are going to encounter in dealing with the masses of population which cannot be raised quickly to the level necessary to produce the results that we want to see.

An additional problem is what I call the constantly proving the-grass-doesn't-grow tendency that we fall into; this is, expecting to see instant results from processes which, common sense should tell us, have to take generations to result. Just to give you some facile, intellectual thinking, I would argue that economic change doesn't just have to produce new middle classes. You don't get the types of thinking characteristic of middle classes until you get the next generation after the new middle classes. I have seen this in Indonesia where the human rights people are telling me they are not getting any support from the new middle classes that are emerging. Why, the new middle classes have just gotten their hands on new things. They are not revolutionary in their thinking. They don't want to challenge the establishment. It's the older middle class that are the ones that begin to insist on having a say in political systems and that become, essentially, the moving force for the types of societal changes that we need to see emerge in these countries in order to bring them closer to our own value system. Well, how do you sustain that process long-gone? You no longer have the Cold War security interests that enabled us to live with repressive, authoritarian regimes in Korea and Taiwan, and in other places in Asia so that they move this process along and then liberalize their system. Without that security justification we are having difficulty dealing with the big countries that are still struggling with this problem. Unless we find a way to intellectualize our ways through this into an understanding of how we need to relate our longer term interests to a strategy of dealing with these countries, instead of letting technical considerations knock us off-course every time they run through one of their constant jolts that they are going to encounter in this process, we are not going to be able to sustain an involvement with Asia that is going to be compatible with our long-term interests in this part of the world.

I would argue that East Asia, because of its geographic and economic development nature, is inherently unstable. You have a giant continental power of China. You have giant world-class small geographic countries such as Japan; you have a very substantial collection of countries in South-east Asia that have never been able to stabilize the situation in the past. As I mentioned, we are in a new era here and Asia has never been a closed region. The balance of power in Asia has always involved the presence of outside powers. And at the moment we are the critical outside power in the region and it is our presence here that essentially has the ability to stabilize this process. Take us out of the region and I guarantee that you will see instability emerging in Asia. For example, it is our presence that helps to stabilize the inherent latent rivalry between China and Japan. You could already see how this rivalry works when the President goes to Japan and you can see China worry about whether we are, in fact, lining up with Japan against China. And Japan worries when you get too close to China. This is why we have to play a balancing role. But to play that balancing role we have to somehow deal with the problem of the overly moralistic approach to countries that aren't going to be able to be compatible with our interests over the next 100 or 150 years perhaps. And we can't use the Washington grass-grow approach to testing whether our approach is working. Now why do I give that example? It is because I read in our number one newspapers in the United States statements such as, "the President broke the linkage with MFN and here it's a year later and we don't see any positive progress." Now I ask you, is that a sensible way to look at the processes that are going to take generations to have any discernible results? If you put water and fertilizer on the grass and then go out and look very carefully for several hours to see whether there are any positive results, conclude that there aren't any and start putting Bromo-Seltzer and sulfuric acid out instead. You are going to have a disastrous lawn. But we seem to think that somehow you can produce rapid change in political systems and respect for human rights because of an economic development process, change that is going to take generations to produce results that we need to see.

So how do we incorporate a better understanding of these processes into our foreign policy and into our domestic political processes so that we can sustain the types of foreign policies that we need to sustain at this current time? We have never previously been successful in maintaining an involvement in the world under the types of circumstances that we are facing now. And the pressure is on us, if you look at our budgetary processes, which are drawing down our engagement. We are closing our diplomatic missions around the world. We are cutting our budgets. Our ability to fund the sorts of things that support our business interests abroad are being cut back. The Asians, despite our agreements with Japan on maintaining our bases there, are all convinced that we are somehow in the process of withdrawing from this region. And yet, we cannot afford to withdraw. It is absolutely inevitable that if we do withdraw further, we will be drawn back into the region by the instabilities that will result and it will require our re-engagement, because this has been the history of the past and it is likely to be the history of the future.

So I would argue that we need to think carefully about how we, as Americans, need to be primed to develop new ways of thinking for dealing with an area of the world that is vitally important to our interests, and that is going through a new phase that requires us to react in new ways. I don't think we are dealing as successfully with that process as we are capable of, and one of the reasons is because this area has been very successful. It is because the current trends are generally positive and therefore we have some time to do the work that needs to be done to incorporate this sort of thinking, if we do it. Is it doable? The answer is yes. Look at Russia. Despite the suppression in Chechnia, our leaders have made for the case, for the American people, that trying to support the process taking place in Russia is so important that we shouldn't be thrown off track by specific aspects of the process that we are fundamentally not too taken with. Why can't we do that in Asia as well? But we haven't made the case to the American people yet and we are constantly struggling to not get thrown off track by the reactions which our own systems generated. And this is something we can think about.

So I would pose for you that the outlook for the United States and Asia is a very positive one if we can know ourselves, understand the region and then find the right policies for dealing with it.

Thank you.

Chapter 15

Japan's Foreign Policy

Yoshio Hatano

President Clinton received an enthusiastic welcome this week in Japan. Japanese newspapers carried favorable articles about his visit, which is not usual in Japan. Assistant Secretary of State Winston Lord called the meeting between the President and our Prime Minister the most successful meeting ever held between the Japanese leader and the United States leader. Why was it so? Because the United States decided to set aside trade problems and concentrate on political issues. As a result, the United States and Japan issued a statement reaffirming the importance and necessity of United States–Japan special relationship including a security treaty. We signed an agreement about Japan's logistic support of the United States. We are going to produce our own domestic law enabling Japan to export weapons to the United States, in spite of the traditional policy of not exporting weapons abroad. Also we are going to enter a joint study about Japan's role in case of hostility in the Pacific. The United States concentrated on the security problems largely because of the Okinawan problem — now fortunately resolved.

There are at least two questions. One, can Japan live up to the expectation of the United States and the world in the security field? Second, what do we do about trade problems? About the first question much depends upon how stable the Japanese government can be in the near future. Japanese political situation is very unstable, even in a state of confusion at the present time. But an encouraging element is that the two main parties, Liberal Democratic Party and New Frontier Party are both led by able leaders in their 50's which is very young by Japanese standards. They seem willing to accept expanded responsibility of Japan in the world.

About the trade field, we now have three problems from the United States side, namely film, semiconductor and insurance. From the Japanese side we would like to revise the Airline Treaty. How do we settle these problems? About two months ago the Japanese Vice-Minister of International Trade and Industry said in a press conference that time of free trade has arrived. The time has come to engage in trade problems multilaterally rather than bilaterally. The New York Times carried an editorial criticizing this remark saying that two friendly countries, the United States and Japan should try to settle problems bilaterally instead of multilaterally. But in the past whenever we gave trade concessions to the United States, Japan was placed under very strong pressure from European countries and some Asian countries, including Australia, that the agreement between our two countries was prejudicial to the interests of other countries; and they opposed the bilateral agreements. As a matter of fact, this morning before I came down to the meeting, I was watching Star Television and I learned that the European Union issued a statement opposing continuation of the semiconductor agreement between Japan and the United States. So we would like to settle trade problems multilaterally and in the forum of the World Trade Organization. Some of my American friends complain that it would take time. That is not necessarily so. I was once Ambassador in Geneva handling GATT programs.

Now, I do not know whether my explanations sound fair to the United States. In fact, two days before I left Tokyo for this meeting, the Editor-in-Chief of Business Week Magazine, Steve Sheppard, interviewed me. He had only one question to ask, this question was: "the United States gives security protection to Japan, what does Japan give in return?" If Mr. Sheppard has some tangible concession from Japan in the field of trade in mind, I have to say, "not much". But Japan will continue to do what it can. Japan will continue to expand its economic assistance program. Japan provided $14 billion of cooperation to developing nations last year. Japan committed $7.7 billion of cooperation to the environmental problem in Rio de Janeiro three years ago to be paid in five years. Two years ago we committed $3 billion of economic cooperation for population programs in a conference in Cairo, during the next five years. We will continue to bear 70 percent of the total cost of United States forces stationed in Japan, while European countries bear about 20 percent for forces stationed in their countries. We will accept Japan's increase in contribution to the United Nations budget from 13 percent to more than 15 percent in the near future. We have participated in UN peace keeping operations in Angola, Mozambique, Zaire and Cambodia and now in the Golan Heights. In cooperating with economic reconstruction of Bosnia, we probably shall be bearing about 10 percent of the total cost. Japan is the chairman country of the environment subcommittee for economic reconstruction of Palestinian area.

South-east Asian countries have anxiety regarding China, because China is expanding its military budget by more than 20 percent every year. China continues nuclear tests. China is reluctant to sign an agreement of complete nuclear test-ban. So there are reasons for South-east Asian countries to have some anxiety. But they also have some anxiety towards Japan. If the United States should leave Japan they are afraid that Japan may re-arm itself. They are afraid that Japan may even go nuclear. So, the result of this President's visit to Japan is welcomed by most South-east Asian countries. I'm not sure if I have answered to the satisfaction of Mr. Sheppard, but I am still confident that Winston Lord is right in saying that it was a most successful visit to Tokyo by President Clinton.

Thank you.

PART IV

PRINCETON PERSPECTIVES

Chapter 16

Princeton and Asia in the Twenty-First Century

Harold Shapiro

Asia in the 21st Century — this was the topic of an Alumni Conference held in Hong Kong this April. The subject is as wide-ranging and complex as the various countries and cultures it embraces, and one that has increasing significance for Princeton's educational and research programs. Vivian and I had the good fortune to participate in the conference and visit with Princeton alumni and friends located in Asia. Presentations drew on the expertise and experience of leaders in their fields. For example, Toyoo Gyohten *56, Chairman of the Bank of Tokyo, spoke on Japan's growing partnership role in Asia. Discussion was led by Princeton Economics Professor Gregory Chow, and alumni including Tsu-Koon Koh '70, Chief Minister of Penang, Malaysia, Gordon Y. S. Wu '58, Managing Director of Hopewell Holdings in Hong Kong, and a panel including Professor Gilbert Rozman *71, Director of the Council on Regional Studies, and Xie Xide, past president of Fudan University, considered social and political change in Asia. An address on U.S. relations by trustee and former U.S. Secretary of State James Baker '52 was followed by discussion among J. Stapleton Roy '56, U.S. Ambassador to Indonesia, L. Desaix Anderson '58, chargé d'affaires, U.S. Embassy in Vietnam and Yoshio Hatano '56, former ambassador to the U.N. from Japan.

The conference had much to teach us. While the often complex questions raised at the conference do not lend themselves to easy solution, the discussions they generated clearly signal the need for deeper understanding between Americans and Asians of each other's cultures and values. Princeton can play and is playing an important role in meeting that need. Most directly, Princeton contributes to this effort through programs in teaching and research. The Department of East Asian Studies has long held a pre-eminent position in instruction and scholarship in this field, and continues to strengthen its offerings. For instance, the department has always considered language mastery as fundamental and recently added courses in Korean. An intensive summer language program begun in 1993 at Beijing Normal University, directed by Professors Chih-Ping Chou and Perry Link, has already gained acclaim.

Teaching and scholarship in areas outside the Department of East Asian Studies, especially in the social sciences, in music, art and religion, also demonstrate significant attention to these topics. For example, students may select from over a dozen history courses related to Asia, ranging from Gyan Prakash's The Making of Modern India to Susan Naquin's course on China,1800 to the Present. Offerings in politics range from a general survey of the politics of Asia to Kent Calder's course on Japanese politics since World War II. Resources such as the Gest Oriental Library, a world-renown collection of reference works on East Asia, contribute significantly to the preeminence of Asian studies at Princeton. The Art Museum's collections in this area provide instruction, cultural insights, and delight for our campus community as well as the general public. At the moment, Wen Fong 51 *58, Edward E. Sanford Professor of Art History and Faculty Curator for Asian Art along with one of his former graduate students, Robert E. Harrist, Jr. *89, is organizing a major exhibition for the Museum devoted to Chinese calligraphy, drawn from the collection of alumnus John B. Elliott '51. The exhibition, scheduled to open in 1999, is intended to educate a wide American audience about Chinese calligraphy, and more broadly, to suggest what this form of communication can tell us about the civilization that created it. Professor Fong was responsible this spring for bringing to the Metropolitan Museum of Art in New York the highly acclaimed exhibition, "Splendors of Imperial China: Treasures from the National Palace Museum, Taipei." The exhibition will travel to museums in Chicago, San Francisco, and Washington, D.C., and I hope some of you will have a chance to see it.

In addition to whatever we may learn from textbooks, from course work, or from the rich collections of our libraries or museum, our understanding of Asia can be enriched through personal contacts with the people of Asia. Indeed, strong and lasting connections between Princeton and Asia depend on the creative energy, passion and dedication of particular individuals. In this respect, our students deserve special attention. Students from Asia (who represent about one-third of all foreign graduate students we admit) bring an added dimension to the life of the University, and, as they pursue careers after graduation here and abroad, they become distinguished ambassadors for Princeton. Asian American members of our community provide a double perspective that bridges East and West. Equally important are opportunities for Princeton students to study or work in Asia, and here, for just under a century, the very successful Princeton-in-Asia program has been a significant resource. The program now annually places about 50 Princeton graduates or student interns in positions as teachers, health workers, journalists, in government and business in countries that include Indonesia, Singapore, Japan, Korea, Thailand, Malaysia, Vietnam, and India. Nearly four percent of Princeton's graduating class now participates in the program.

Looking ahead to the 21st century, among all of the uncertainties, one point seems clear — that our world is shrinking and interdependence among all countries is growing. If our students are to graduate with the skills necessary to serve our society with distinction, they must understand and appreciate other societies. Our intention is to continue and to enhance efforts that foster opportunities to learn from each other so that our students will be better equipped to meet the challenges and benefit from the potential of our interlocking futures.

Chapter 17

Alumni Gather in Hong Kong to Discuss Asia's Future

Luther T. Munford

Hong Kong — The Alumni Council held one of its most successful regional conferences ever in Hong Kong on April 19–20. Titled "Asia in the 21st Century", the conference drew 300 alumni from 17 nations to a two-day discussion of the economic and political future of Asia and the role of the United States there.

The conference was the first Princeton regional conference ever held outside the United States. It kicked off a series of conferences the Alumni Council is sponsoring to celebrate the University's 250th anniversary. The Alumni Council decided to hold the conference in Hong Kong to promote the anniversary theme: "Princeton in the Nation's Service and in the Service of All Nations". The conference also honored the increasingly international nature of the Council's operations. Today 30 of Princeton's 150 regional associations are located outside the United States. In fact, Alumni Council Associate Director Doug Blair '71, who organized the conference, went to Bangkok on his way home to help inaugurate our newest association, the Princeton Alumni Association of Thailand.

The Hong Kong conference included principal addresses by four speakers, as well as three panel discussions. Toyoo Gyohten *56, chairman of the Bank of Tokyo and president of the Princeton Club of Japan, concisely and forthrightly described what he believes is needed for Asian economic development. Gordon Y. S. Wu '58, managing director of Hopewell Holdings Limited and president of the Princeton Club of Hong Kong, discussed the future of Hong Kong and the Peoples' Republic of China. Trustee James A. Baker III '52, former U.S. Secretary of State, outlined strategic considerations in diplomacy for China, Japan and the United States. Finally, President Harold T. Shapiro *63, analyzed the historical relationship between economic growth and technological supremacy.

Questions discussed included the following:

*Will the 21st century be the "Century of Asia"?** Toyoo Gyohten pointed out that U.S. trans-Pacific trade now exceeds its trans-Atlantic trade by 50%. He sees promise in the high economic growth rates, high savings rates, and work ethic of the Asian countries. James Baker speculated that China could well be on its way to being the great power of the world. He also urged that Japan be given an opportunity to play a political role more in keeping with its economic might, and specifically endorsed giving Japan a seat on the U.N. Security Council.

Two panelists, however, pointed out that Asia still has tremendous poverty. Nicholas C. Hope *75, World Bank director for China and Mongolia, said that in East Asia, more people are living in poverty than in sub-Sahara Africa. Barry Metzger '66, general counsel of the Asian Development Bank, made a similar comparison and observed that the Chinese will have great difficulty dealing with an estimated 100 million people likely to be displaced from Chinese agriculture in the next 10 years.

Finally, all agreed that social and political stability is essential to future Asian development, and that both regional institutions and a continued U.S. presence are essential to that stability. Former Japanese Ambassador Yoshio Hatano '56, who came to Hong Kong immediately after participating in the Japanese summit with President Bill Clinton, described that summit as one of the most useful the two countries had ever had because of its focus on security issues.

*What will happen to Hong Kong when the British leave in 1997?** Gordon Wu, for one, is optimistic. He quipped: "What will happen after 1997? 1998." He believes that the Chinese people now recognize that the "goodies" in life come from hard work, not from fighting. He sees a future for Hong Kong's six million people providing economic and other services to China's 1.2 billion people. James Baker takes a more tempered view. As he put it, China is not going to kill the goose that laid the golden egg, i.e. Hong Kong capitalism, but he doubts China knows how to keep the goose from getting sick. Any Beijing crackdown on freedoms in Hong Kong will inevitably hurt tourism and foreign trade there, he believes.

***Will capitalism take hold in Vietnam?** Vietnam has declared a policy of "market socialism". L. Desaix Anderson, Jr. '58, charge d'affaires at the U.S. Embassy there, said that when he arrived in Vietnam he went from embassy to embassy and found that each embassy believed Vietnam was following that country's economic "model", except for the Japanese, who believed there was no foreign model. Anderson agrees with the Japanese. Since 1989, the Vietnamese economy has been growing rapidly. A majority of the "non-governmental organizations" in the country are U.S.-backed. The Vietnamese, however, are worried about "cultural pollution". One morning, Hanoi awoke to find all Coca-Cola and Samsung signs had been painted over.

***Does international education matter?** Michigan State University professor Gill-Chin Lim *78 argued that more Asian students need to come to the U.S., and more U.S. students need to study in Asia. The two cultures, he pointed out, need to understand that they approach matters in totally different ways, which is illustrated by differences as simple as whether a family name goes first, as in Asia, or last, as in the West. Princeton has missed some opportunities in international outreach. Bae Ho Hahn *71, president of the Sejoing Institute in Korea, pointed out that Princeton has failed to capitalize in Korea on the fact that the founder of the modern Korean State, Syngman Rhee *10, held a Princeton graduate degree. Progress, however, is being made elsewhere. Princeton admitted 11 applicants from Singapore this year and

8 from Hong Kong. Gordon Wu observed that the Asian leaders with whom he now deals frequently have been educated in the United States, and he finds it encouraging that, of the students sent to study abroad by the P.R.C., at least one-third return.

John T. Kamm '72, a California businessman active in human rights issues, offered a joke on this subject. It seems that a mother mouse walking with her child was confronted by a cat. The mother mouse raised up on her hind legs and barked like a dog: "Wuff." The cat scurried away. "That," the mother mouse explained to her child, "is the value of learning a second language."

The value of international education is also demonstrated by conferences like this one that allow a free interchange of ideas among alumni with both a vision of the world's future and a voice in how that future will be shaped.